CONVERSATIONS WITH
MICHAEL EIGEN

CONVERSATIONS WITH MICHAEL EIGEN

Michael Eigen and Aner Govrin

KARNAC

First published in 2007 by
Karnac Books Ltd
118 Finchley Road, London NW3 5HT

British Library Cataloguing in Publication Data

A C.I.P. for this book is available from the British Library

ISBN 978 1 85575 550 5

Edited, designed and produced by The Studio Publishing Services Ltd
www.publishingservicesuk.co.uk
e-mail: studio@publishingservicesuk.co.uk

Printed in Great Britain

10 9 8 7 6 5 4 3 2 1

www.karnacbooks.com

CONTENTS

ABOUT THE AUTHORS

Michael Eigen is the author of sixteen books and many papers. His most recent works include *Feeling Matters; Lust; Emotional Storm;* and *Age of Psychopathy*. He is a senior member of the National Psychological Association for Psychoanalysis and is on the faculty of the New York University Postdoctoral Program for Psychotherapy and Psychoanalysis. He has been providing private seminars on Bion, Winnicott, and Lacan in New York City for the past thirty years.

Aner Govrin, PhD, is a clinical psychologist in private practice in Tel Aviv, and is on the faculty of the Department of Hermeneutics at Bar-Ilan University. He is a member of the Tel Aviv Institute for Contemporary Psychoanalysis and the International Association of Relational Psychoanalysis and Psychotherapy. His book, *Between Abstinence and Seduction – The Analysis of American Psychoanalysis* (Dvir), was published in 2004 in Hebrew.

Books by Michael Eigen

Karnac publications

The Psychotic Core (1986, 2004)
The Electrified Tightrope (ed. Adam Phillips) (1993, 2004)
Psychic Deadness (1996, 2004)
Toxic Nourishment (1999)
Damaged Bonds (2001)
Feeling Matters (2007)

Other publications

Coming Through the Whirlwind (1992)
Reshaping the Self (1995)
The Psychoanalytic Mystic (1998)
Ecstasy (2001)
Rage (2002)
The Sensitive Self (2004)
Emotional Storm (2005)
Lust (2006)
Age of Psychopathy (2007)

INTRODUCTION

Aner Govrin

These lively conversations provide a unique insight into the mind of one of the most original psychoanalysts. The various subjects covered here spread over a wide range of interests which Michael Eigen talks about in a rich and almost ecstatic flow. Eigen's writing so closely resembles Eigen's talking that a conversation book is almost necessary. My hope is that it will enable readers to enter the ideas of Eigen more directly than she or he could have via Eigen's books and papers.

The first part of the conversation focuses on Eigen's psychoanalytic thought; the second part concentrates on his personal life; and the third includes supervision which he undertook on two cases from my clinic: a patient convinced that she and I were having a love affair and a young woman who thought, in the midst of therapy, that she was chosen by God to fulfil a holy mission.

This book does not intend to answer all the questions the reader might have wanted to put to Michael Eigen. It can only provide possible directions to some of Eigen's more intriguing ideas, such as the place of Light and God in psychotherapy, the multiple self, or the sense of living and deadness.

My talks with Michael Eigen took place between September and December, 2003, in his clinic in Manhattan and in his Brooklyn home. We had seven conversations, which lasted more than twenty hours. After leaving America I continued to correspond with Eigen in order to elaborate his expressed thoughts.

I like to think that Michael Eigen's poetic books—*Rage, Ecstasy, The Sensitive Self, Emotional Storm*, and *Lust*—represent a new turn in psychoanalysis. Since Jung, no author has allied psychoanalysis with God and the mystic as much as Eigen does. No psychoanalytic writer has dared to say that "psychoanalysis is a form of prayer" (1998, p. i) or urged his readers "to love God with all your heart, soul, might and to feel the heartbreak at the center of existence, and the deeper joy, working within the storm, in the feel of feelings, the feel of life, the feel of one's life" (2005a).

But Eigen is much more than a psychoanalytic mystic. He is aiming for a new phenomenology, one capable of making the therapist/writer mesh with the world without reflecting on it from the outside. In one of his paradoxical allegories, Borges, imagined an empire in which the art of Cartography had gained such perfection that a map was exactly the same size as the area it depicted. Michael Eigen's attempts to mirror experience from the inside, to practise a peculiar form of correspondence to experience (in contrast to correspondence to reality), runs the risk of reaching a similar condition. His words do not represent, stand for, or analyse from a distance, but rather authentically convey many living moments. He talks about the psyche on a scale, the proportion of which is so small that it gives you the feeling of a dense colourful kaleidoscope. With every turn, fresh bits and pieces of experiential reality reveal themselves. Eigen speaks psychoanalysis in a way that breathes. Like Rabbi Akivah, one of his beloved figures, he hungers for everything that proceeds out of the mouth of God.

Ever since he began writing, Eigen has been preoccupied with areas of experience largely unknown or neglected in daily life. What contact could persons establish with their inner self that has not been opened yet? Why do persons wilfully shut their eyes and their mind to a stormy area? How can a person stay with the terror, resonance, hate, beauty of inner and exterior life? "One feels impelled", he writes in *Emotional Storm*, "to bring to awareness still neglected, denied, or undervalued realms of being, on the chance that telling stories in one's own way will touch the lives of others" (2005b, p. 80,). A good way to describe what Eigen tries to do is to cite his words on Rilke (*ibid.*, pp. 75–76). Eigen (like Rilke) "seems wholly bent on letting experience speak, holding on to nothing, giving himself to the impact of the moment, as it builds, transforms, opens, shatters . . ." He opens his heart to

> anguish, terror, beauty, to the trauma of the sensitivity, to the impact of love/no love, the impact of time, presence/absence, the impact of sensitivity itself. He is so sensitive to sensitivity. He alerts us to give the world to itself by transforming it—precisely by letting it impact inside us, letting impact incubate, visible become invisible, swirling, dropping into dreamwork, poet-work, alpha function—passing through psychic digestive systems, tasting, transmuting experience, psychical beings working like new kinds of worms. [*ibid.*]

In his writings, Eigen is not as interested in finding new psychoanalytic explanations for interesting clinical phenomena, as most writers in this field. Similarly, he is not entirely interested in the reader's understanding. The main thing is not to be factual and sound but illuminating. Texts are not academically produced, but splash out of the mind in an emotional and visionary autobiographical blend. It's no wonder his poetic books have no references. The absence of references is meaningful. It represents a progressive shift from psychoanalytic knowledge based on rational argumentations supported by previous knowledge to writing about raw experiences in a poetic manner. A reference will make the reader pause and might lead to a decline in the author–reader movement. A reference is a strident pause within the text. The absence of references is a change of register in the writer's discourse. Eigen barely uses psychoanalytic jargon. Psychoanalytic jargon gives an exterior form to inner life, to raw experience, conscious and unconscious. What seems for Eigen to be more important is the felt realization that we are alive, precious, amazing, thrilling, capable of injury, joy, caring. He is interested in the immediate, positive, apprehension of reality (2005b, p. 185).

Eigen's writing has a feel, a tempo, a sense of rhythm. He injects into his texts something puzzling, a surprising melody, and the reader gets used to a "no business-as-usual" atmosphere. Eigen refuses to be boxed in, or easily packaged. Instead, he keeps his readers in tune with what he values most: "freshness of being, the taste of experience, the shock of aliveness" (*ibid.*, p. 105).

His books are not continuous or cumulative, but consist of separate "tastes" of experiential moments. His texts are missing the ordinary sequence of a-point-leads-to-a-point. Instead his writings are a mixture of semi-visionary experiences, poetic experimentations, psychoanalytic essays, thoughts on the Bible, poetry, and literature, autobiographical memories, case studies, works of mysticism, and radical images of society and politics. It moves fast from one sphere to another. Is he writing psychoanalysis? Poetry? Does he try to tell us something new about conflict, rage, sensitivity? Share with us his personal story? These unclear questions make the reader alert, unready, finding it hard to foresee the next step.

I wrote elsewhere (Govrin, 2007) that Eigen's prose is a radical experiment that tests whether it is possible to do what Bion suggests—create a language that has an indescribable, incomprehensible, yet deeply and strongly felt impact, not immediately registered by the reader's conscious processes; a language that attempts to convey experiences "not yet formalized or formulated" (Eigen, 1998, p. 83). I called this kind of engagement between writer and reader an "open reading system". This reading is a risk-taking activity, fully open to experience, which involves some destruction of the reader's pre-existing world, as well as some contact with a real outside world, a real other. In a closed reading system, the main function of the text is communication. Its aim is to convey ideas, descriptions, facts, from one person to another in written form. Most of the texts we read in daily life are closed. When the subject is within the orbit of projective-introjective operations, objects are not experienced as exterior, but as confirming something that already exists within them. This is exactly what Eigen wants to avoid. He wants his readers to connect with a real sense of something outside them, a place that is unfamiliar, strange and difficult to navigate. It is not intended to meet the reader's expectations or to be fully grasped by the reader. Like a stanza of the American poet Mark Strand in "Dark Harbor": "I am writing from a place you have never been" (1994, p. 7), Eigen takes his readers to unfamiliar spheres. This in contrast to writing that leads readers to places where they have already been, echoing something that can be known. The relation Eigen forms with his readers reflects Eigen's understanding of Winnicott's use of the object. Eigen (1993) tells us that for the baby "it is the projective world that is continuously destroyed at the same time that the real is continuously born and vice versa, and both of these happenings are necessary for the real as such to be experienced" (*ibid.*, p. 115). This is also true for a reader in an open reading system. By experiencing the text as incomprehensible, obscure, beyond his grasp, the reader acknowledges that the writer is outside his omnipotent control. Over and over again he feels the text changing his expectations, and occasionally destroying them.

In beautiful lines like "What would we be like without light? / Where could we go to get away from it? / Can one hide from it in a restaurant, going out to dinner with one's wife? / Taste buds open to more than food / Light dances around the table" (Eigen, 2004, p. 142), the text strips away the reader's mind, and the reader is faced with a real other.

At the same time that Eigen's texts are exterior to the reader's mind, they also echo the reader's deepest voices. Eigen's poetic and clinical texts enable readers to make contact with deep areas they value or cannot quite reach or articulate, areas bordering on unknown ability, yet extremely valuable.

There's a challenge, though. The communicative channel itself becomes a challenge. Perhaps, on a deep level, that's what made me interview him. I wanted to understand his creative mind, perhaps be part of it, meet the challenge. But as I started meeting Eigen I soon came to realize that talking to him, like reading him, is a transformative experience. If you want to "understand" a therapeutic method which is embedded in an integrated and structured world view, Michael Eigen is the last psychoanalyst you would think to interview. When you hear Eigen's voice, you soon realize that for him it is the "thing itself" that matters: mere experience, unstructured ideas, rich streams of thoughts, ceaseless movement, a feeling of biblical flood or a rainbow.

As with his books, his listeners have to transform their attentive capacities. During our first sessions I asked Eigen to explain ideas or notions which were enigmatic for me: "Just what do you mean by that? Would you mind saying it again? Sorry, I couldn't catch up." At first Eigen politely cooperated, but soon he got tired and began to moan and complain. He asked me to let go. He certainly did not want to be interrupted. But I could not resist the temptation of understanding it all. I assumed that I could superimpose my own categories of thoughts on his world. I wanted to navigate in his world without getting lost. But it was no use. I got lost again and again. It took me a while to understand that in my attempts to find *my* way in *his* thoughts, I am missing much of the surprise, beauty, and living moments of the conversation. It is as if we were in a beautiful green meadow, Eigen showing me rare and colourful butterflies. I wanted us to catch each butterfly, dissect it, and examine it so we could fully analyse it. But Eigen insisted: let them fly, let them be free.

As time passed, I learned to enjoy my unknowingness. Instead of making efforts to "understand" what Eigen meant, I began experiencing feelings and thoughts his voice stimulated in my own mind. I began to interact with Eigen in a real experiential sense. Eigen's words were cues to a rich stream of thought that took place in my own conscious and unconscious world. I began to meditate while he talked. I now believe that this is the best way to read Eigen.

There was another subject that made me curious. Eigen likes to share with his readers intimate details about his personal life, including intimate stories about his childhood, adolescence, parents, and sexual experiences. No one has ever done that before in the secretive and discrete psychoanalytic community. Most writers prefer to draw a sharp line between the personal and the theoretical. Even our most intimate patients, whom we know for years, know very little about us. Only in the past ten years has analytic self disclosure been discussed openly. But even this discussion has been restricted to the therapeutic dyad, neglecting the author–reader dyad. Eigen's own self-disclosure reflects the most basic premise of psychoanalysis: everything we do (or write) is part of our autobiography. In fact, his many biographical descriptions (including analysis of his homosexual dreams) constitute a rehabilitation and revival of Freud's self-analysis. However, Eigen has something else on his mind. He is less interested in the mechanism that lies behind the psyche, but rather wants to communicate his insights in the most direct way and to practise openness to experience. Eigen knows that hiding the subjectivity of the author behind psychoanalytic jargon kills the text and blocks living moments and creativity. Eigen's autobiographical descriptions are so mixed with his patients, biblical and Shakespearian characters, that without change of pronoun it would be difficult for the reader to decide who the subject of the text is.

In reality, though, Eigen is private and shy. The "me" is less important than the stream of free associations, day-dreaming, and opening paths to the most basic feelings. He is particularly sensitive to his privacy when he speaks about God. In one of our sessions I felt I intruded on his privacy when I asked him whether he believed in God. For Eigen the question was just too much. "Everything I have to say about God is written in my books," he said, dryly. As the meeting ended, Eigen gave me a ride from his Brooklyn house to the nearest subway. It was a glorious Brooklyn night and the sky was rich with stars. It was quite chilly outside but warm inside the car. I thought about the Light. It was out there, somewhere. Eigen is usually eager to share his thoughts with his listeners. This time he drove in silence. He seemed preoccupied with his own world. The car stopped in the parking lot near the subway. Neither of us made a move. Everything stopped for a short moment. I broke the silence and said: "Perhaps the notion of God is too intimate and sacred for you that you don't feel you can share it with me." Eigen put his hand on my shoulder in a fatherly gesture. He had a soft and gentle touch. "That's true," he said. "It's very sensitive of you to understand that." At that moment all was good and right. During my ride home I felt raw happiness, faith in the goodness of living. A paragraph from *The Sensitive Self*, which I later read, reminds me of those feelings: "When I got home," Sara tells Eigen, her therapist, "I felt the warmth, faith, shattered heart of your song—a sun inside me."

References

Govrin, A. (2007). The area of faith between Eigen and his readers, *Quadrant: Journal of the C.G. Jung Foundation for Analytical Psychology*, 37(1): 9–27.

Eigen, M. (1993). *The Electrified Tightrope*. London: Karnac, 2004.

Eigen, M. (1998). *The Psychoanalytic Mystic*. London: Free Association.

Eigen, M. (2004). *The Sensitive Self*. Middletown, CT: Wesleyan University Press.

Eigen, M. (2005a). Personal communication.

Eigen, M. (2005b). *Emotional Storm*. Middletown: Wesleyan University Press.

Strand, M. (1994). Dark Harbor: A Poem. New York: Knopf.

"My sense of the holy has a positive and a negative source. The positive is the holiness of life and of human life. The negative is the awakening that comes from seeing the inevitability of injury and the wish to work with, struggle with our nature. The holiness of therapy involves, in part, a practical application of this struggle with life to release life, to make life better. With me, the sense of holiness also has a sense of feeling free, connected, home: working with the human psyche as a kind of home. An odd kind of home, since we don't feel at home there, a homeless home. But home none the less."

Michael Eigen

"There is no end. There is no beginning. There is only the infinite passion of life."

Federico Fellini

CHAPTER ONE

Thoughts

God

A *ner*:   In *The Psychoanalytic Mystic*, you wrote that therapy is holy and that there are moments when psychoanalysis is a form of prayer. To most analysts these sentences might seem strange. Segregation between these two worlds—spiritualism and psychoanalysis—is the normative analytic stance. What personal experiences have led you to think that way?

Mike: For me these two worlds coincide. The first session I did as a therapist was like breathing fresh air. I felt like a fish in water. Finally, something natural, a fit, and a medium I could be in. It was a blessing after trying so many things—something that felt just right. I was nearly thirty and had worked as a therapist with children at camps, schools and treatment centres in my mid-twenties. That's part of what got me interested in going more deeply into the therapy field.

I worked at other jobs too, too many to mention. Office work, restaurants, playing in bands, teaching. While teaching at a school for disturbed children, an incident occurred that made me determined to be my own boss. A boy brought in pheasants as gifts from a hunting trip with his father. My supervisor, the head teacher, lectured him about the evil of killing animals and wouldn't accept the gift. I piped up and said to the boy, "Hey, that's great, John. I'd love one." This boy's dad never did anything with him. How great they went hunting, did something together. The boy came in proud and generous and got shot down, shamed. My supervisor went on harping about how bad it was to gratuitously take life. I knew, in an instant, my days in institutional settings were numbered. Soon afterwards, I began graduate school to start work on my doctorate, to work towards greater freedom.

The shock woke me. People could treat animals with sanctity yet be sanctimoniously cruel to humans in their care. By the time I left the school I knew about my supervisor's trauma history and difficulties he faced. I understood more about the risk people take in seeking help. Anything can be used as an excuse by a care-giver to unleash injury. Injury was inflicted and the care-giver felt morally right about it. I realized no one is exempt, and that this risk will apply to people in my care all my life. No one is outside of what we do to each other, for better, for worse. So my sense of holy has a positive and a negative source. The positive is the holiness of life and of human life. The negative is the awakening that comes from seeing the inevitability of injury and the wish to work with, struggle with, our nature. The holiness of therapy involves, in part, a practical application of this struggle with life to release life, to make life better. With me, the sense of holiness also has a sense of feeling free, connected, home: working with the human psyche as a kind of home.

Time is sacred. You and I are meeting during the Rosh Hashanah season and I was thinking that Rosh Hashanah is a Day of Remembrance. So, what are we supposed to remember? Who is supposed to remember what? There are passages in the Bible in which God seems to wake up. God comes to, suddenly remembers his obligations, His contract with His people, His mercy, His loving kindness. As if man wakes God and makes God remember we are here. We wake God in all sorts of ways, but one of the most effective is to cry out, to have nothing left but a cry. The turning point of the Passover Seder is our crying out to God and God hears us. A cry from the heart opens God's heart.

Aner: So it is God who should remember?

Mike: God remembers. He is here and we are here. God awakens to Himself, remembers Himself. "I am here!", as if God was dozing in a fog and suddenly is called to remember. God thinks, "People are calling me." Calling wakes us and wakes God too.

To reverse the projection, one could say that one goes through life not fully awake. There are different kinds of awakeness. Freud's Wolf-Man felt he had a veil over his soul. There is sound-proofing, psyche-proofing, an opacity surrounding the sense of contact. In this context, Rosh Hashanah is remembering that we are here, that we are alive. Waking up to aliveness, becoming alive to our aliveness. Rosh Hashanah tells us to remember that we are human. We are called upon to remember our existence, our relations to ourselves and other people. Thus the Shofar is a wake up call to remind us that we are alive and time is sacred.

Aner: I still don't understand why therapy is a holy thing?

Mike: You keep asking me why when the reality is: it feels that way to me.

Aner: Do you believe in God?

Mike: Everything I have to say about God is written in my books. Yes. But then something whispers maybe I don't believe in God. Maybe I'm agnostic or atheist. Maybe all three. Maybe I'm always all three, a believer, an agnostic, an atheist. Is a final decision necessary? I wonder if part of what I mean by therapy without rigid definition applies to this question, too. To be a questioner is important. To be a critic, a questioner. To be ignorant. Does one have to sacrifice this need if one also feels God? Does one have to sign on a dotted line? Faith is very important to me. I don't cling to it. It is something that happens in my life. It is something that makes itself known to me. Must I also be a believer, subscribe to a literal belief system? I have done that for periods but found it does not work for me. Faith works. Belief in a concrete God system is another matter. I learn from concrete God systems, even am inspired by them. But faith is beyond or other or more than these categories. It comes to me, partly, through a precious feeling, immediate. It can be triggered by many things, a face, a gesture, a thought, a colour, an agony. But it also comes of its own accord, a grace, lifting life, touching life with wonder, a thrill.

Every time I say one thing, others come. Aren't we that way, impossible to get to the bottom?

God does not distinguish between words and silence. In *Moses and Monotheism*, Freud calls the Jewish God a volcano god. Only death silenced Freud's flow of words. But his was the kind of flow that ignites the flow of others. Look, just when the Freud embers appeared to be on the verge of dying, book after book flares up from this or that bit of his work. Freud could not stop talking about religion. Partly because it was his way of continuing his talk with Jung, an inner contact he could not cancel; partly because he was affirming science over religion; and partly because he could not stop talking with the Jewish God.

To be alive

Aner: What does it mean to forget that one is alive?

Mike: I think every one forgets that he or she is alive and goes through life semi-sleepwalking, in a somewhat hypnotic and hallucinatory state. A lot of life involves shared hallucinations. A lot of fights involve antagonistic hallucinations. Writings on schizoid and borderline personalities are about people who don't feel alive or feel too alive or alive in the wrong way. Many have lost their sense of aliveness, more or less. I write about our varying sense of aliveness–deadness in *Psychic Deadness*.

You wonder how it is possible to lose your sense of aliveness and to still be alive. To be alive in order to say: I am not alive, or I am alive in some ways but not in others, alive somewhat. Schreber, a judge who became psychotic and wrote about it, describes a blackout when self and world disappear or die, and then the world gets "miracle'd up", re-created through hallucination. Freud wrote a beautiful essay based on Schreber's autobiography. Freud never treated Schreber, but his work about the latter is a masterpiece. He raises the possibility that hallucination is a way of re-creating a lost or destroyed other, a lost world returned in another key. Out of depersonalization and deadness, a new universe, a psychotic rebirth process begins. Aliveness returns in a semi-erotic, paranoid, attacking mode. I tried to bring out structures and dynamics of

Schreber's journey and Freud's descriptions in Chapter Seven of *The Psychotic Core*. You might say it is an account of holiness run amok, the sense of holiness in a paranoid context.

Now, even when one is dead, one struggles to come alive. For many people, the sense of being dead acts as a disturbance that drives them towards life, often unsuccessfully. One falls back trapped in deadness, behind the veil. But disturbance pushes one to try again, as if there is a tropism towards life, and death makes one restless. The schizoid individual flattens or cuts off emotion, as if emotion chronically is drained away, like blood that has been drawn out.

Aner: How can it be possible that there is a mix of aliveness and deadness in the same person?

Mike: That is a very good question and we don't know. Many writers have written about dehumanization and depersonalization in our world: T. S. Elliot's "The Waste Land", and "The Hollow Men", Heidegger's writings on the machine and the need for poetry, Ortega Y Gasset on art and dehumanization, aspects of Beckett's work. One could go on and on. Deadness, emptiness, meaninglessness, as well as madness, have been important themes of art and literature in the twentieth century. Destruction wreaked by wars complemented them. Critiques of the structure of modern life multiplied. Marx targeted the worker's alienation from the products and profits he contributed to. Weber spoke of a "secular asceticism" accruing to the Protestant work ethic. Spengler wrote of the receding of intuitive man in favour of economic man and has a chapter on money in *The Decline of the West*.

Our words are misleading. In chemistry, doesn't mixture mean materials that can be brought together and separated out again? Is that what we mean by coincidence or co-existence of deadness–aliveness? Perhaps it's easier to tease out alive and dead areas in a tree—after all, a tree can be alive and have dead or dying areas. Maybe people studying the brain can discover the chemistry/neurology underlying the sense of aliveness–deadness. Then again, chemistry and organ function vary with environmental impacts.

Aner: Could you say more about hyper-stimulation as a sign of aliveness?

Mike: Winnicott wrote about people keeping themselves in aliveness because they are afraid to drop out of aliveness or fear aliveness will drop away and they will be stranded in—what? Nothing? Emptiness? Deadness? Nowhere? Something worse? Unrepresentable agonies beyond agonies.

Aner: Aliveness will drop away and one will no longer be a person. One will lose the capacity to be a person who is in life.

Mike: One will reach the point of no return and enter the beyond where there is no link with life, no connection. Gone. As therapists, as people, we are learning a lot about "gone." A way of saying this, too, is that the heart of the past stopped beating. A broken heart, we say. But often it is more than broken: warped, poisoned, strangulated, and pulverized. We like words like arrested development, frozen self, catastrophe, and permanent shock. There are many formulations of deadness now. We know more and more about it. We begin to perceive cultural dimensions to it too, the violence of civilization. Now our focus is on war and terrorism and corporate violence. Trauma and upheaval is a constant in our lives, part of the brew that makes up life. Whether or not we can exist any other way remains to be seen.

A clinical example Winnicott gives near the end of his transitional object paper is of a woman who had to be a transitional object for her mother in order to keep her mother in life. This woman did not have the freedom to drop out of life. She couldn't just drop into nothing or chaos. She had to keep reviving up existence to keep her mother in life. It is natural to take time off, to leave, to vacate, and to become unintegrated. To maintain oneself as an integrated unit, a hyper-integrated unit, can become artificial. This woman pumped herself up for her mother's benefit, a kind of psychic oxygen pump for her mother. It is natural to drop in and out of being a person, to take vacations from oneself for a time. Perhaps this is another aspect of a basic rhythm I describe in *The Sensitive Self*.

Some of Winnicott's best clinical portrayals involved setting up conditions in which people can drop out. One gets the hang of dropping in and out: of oneself, of presence, of absence. In *Playing and Reality*, he tells of giving a woman open-ended sessions that could go on and on until she felt ready to stop. What enabled her to stop was reaching towards a state of unintegration, dropping out of her usual self-organization into chaos; a safe freshness that enables her re-forming and un-forming. I'm tempted to call it "oiling the hinges", except there are no hinges, no door.

It is a paradoxical moment or dimensionality. Drifting into nothingness, chaos, meaninglessness, unintegration where meaningful experience emerges. To let go into formlessness is itself meaningful for one who chronically maintains life by self-gripping or pushing. In a related way, Bion spoke of meaning becoming meaningful if one is able to let go of meaning, if one can also experience meaninglessness. A bit like the contrast full–empty, a real aspect of an infant's feeding at the breast.

Aner: It is possible the kind of session Winnicott described might end with something emotionally meaningful growing out of chaos, fresh contact after letting contact go.

Mike: It might also end savouring relief at not having to force oneself to be. To be free of having to be this or that version of oneself, time off from personality. Chaos and nothingness as welcome, not merely terrifying, visitors. Winnicott's sense of unintegration has something in common with Berdyaev's "neonic freedom" and Sartre's *pour soi*, the open nothingness of consciousness. What I am terming "neo-plasticity".

Aner: What sort of feeling is this?

Mike: Would you ask what does being horny feel like? Is it possible to take a vacation from oneself, from one's performativity, from one's tie to particular images? Is it possible not to experience my desire through another's? Can one breathe without pressuring another to think of one in a certain way? Can I only keep myself in life by enlivening someone's desire? Do these imaginary scenes always have the last word? Is there another word? Wordlessness? A hiatus, chasm? Are Hindus wrong to place so much on the pendulum rhythm of breath, the gap, the stop after each swing, after each in or out?

Aner: Can someone live like that forever?

Mike: Forever? It's not hard enough living it for a moment in a session? Once one tastes the possibility of vacating in a positive way (contradiction in terms?) one finds ability to take off from oneself more often during the day, mini-vacations, even in sessions. It's a matter of growth of capacity. Of making room for not being there as well as being there. Developing a better rhythm in one's feel for life.

Guntrip–Winnicott

Mike: Guntrip spoke of not being able to just be, an inability to let activity go. He hoped his analysis with Winnicott would give him a taste of letting down control. Guntrip was a doer rather than a be'er. He came to Winnicott, partly, to taste this missing capacity. It's like someone having to be on stage all the time, not being able to be off stage. Guntrip got a taste or vision of less defensive being through the kind of attentiveness Winnicott offered.

This therapy couple has been harshly criticized for not going far enough, not dealing with hidden aggression, creating a mutual appreciation society. I doubt if Guntrip would have been able to work with many of these critics. There are certain borderline and narcissistic patients who will not allow themselves to go very far in therapy if they feel the therapist is too alien, too normal perhaps, too "analytic", too out of reach with regard to—let's call it a basic vision of self or life, a feel for things. Guntrip emphasized a schizoid aspect, a way of being out of contact, withdrawn, perhaps to preserve a modicum of core self-feeling, perhaps out of fear that contact would be devastating or somehow take one's sense of self away. Perhaps there is not a firm enough sense of the restorative, resilient nature of interaction, a rhythm of injury, recovery, growth, a lived dialectical happening. One gets set on not being there, living life out of the corners of being, peeking at the enemy, or simply closing one's eyes. Some of these people need a sense of felt agreement on a very deep level, a profound cohering or overlapping of vision of self as valued, precious, and sacred. It is a feeling emitted and transmitted self-to-self. Call it symbiosis, fusion, collusion—whatever you like. But it is real. At its centre is a belief, a conviction—no, more: a sensation of the holiness of self, a sense of quality, something of intrinsic worth or value. I think Guntrip and Winnicott read this agreement in each other's beings, a core-to-core respect and caring. It is this that made work between them possible, with whatever limitations. This core "agreement" does not preclude differences. Winnicott never gave up his sense that Guntrip was too goody-goody, that sadism and aggressiveness was part of the self, part of basic aliveness. But he worked with what he was given, as conditions allowed and, I suppose, did the best that he dared or could. It may be this shared vision of quality of self militated against a full range of aggressive expressiveness. But it also played a role in allowing what could happen to happen. Without it there would have been no therapy at all.

I have seen the opposite happen, all too often. The analyst interprets the patient's hostility, sexual defences, controlling, evasive, manipulative, and seductive activities, while the precious core self is pushed aside. Gains are made but there are important ways in which the self remains pinched, contracted, smaller. In Guntrip's case, there were limitations perhaps, but a sense of core self opened more.

Aner: Did Winnicott and Guntrip share the same experience?

Mike: Yes, in the sense of a dedicated respect and caring for a sacred core self. But they had real differences. Guntrip felt aggression was reactive to maternal failure. Winnicott felt aggression was a constitutive tendency of the self, part of self-feeling, part of the aliveness of self, taking different forms, partly and importantly, but not exclusively, tied to environmental response. This difference was never resolved. And there were personality differences as well. The basic shared agreement did not nullify difference.

Aner: Harry Guntrip described himself as a person who felt intense doubleness.

Mike: Yes, Guntrip lived a full, rich life but also had a dead core, wholly dead in one way, wholly alive in another, a foot in deadness, a foot in aliveness, so to speak. The two indistinguishably compressed, melded; but different enough to elicit agonized perception of the difference. To be alive *and* to be dead: not just a continuum, not just polarities. Life spots, death spots: the same place. Guntrip had an uncanny sense, an acute sensitivity to aliveness and deadness, their co-presence, fluctuations, intermingling. He tried to split the deadness off, circumscribe or localize it, keep it tucked in place. That was one reason he was drawn to Fairbairn.

Fairbairn knew about splitting. He knew about deadness and perhaps felt that deadness resulted from splitting, from attacks upon aliveness, a sealing-off, delimiting process. The reverse plays a role as well, deadness occasioning splitting, as if trying to simulate, stimulate an internal murderer to raise hell, to enliven through deforming self-attack. The deforming life-attacker Fairbairn called an "internal saboteur".

Guntrip felt his work with Winnicott somewhat more satisfactory. Winnicott didn't try to "localize" the deadness but saw it as part of primary maternal deficit. He thought it was an emotive lack that was part of the nutrient field that Guntrip grew in, not only a negative presence, but something missing; the deadness as an index of not just freezing or going dead as a result of being attacked or dropped, but part of a missing emotion, a deadening lack in the emotional world that succoured him. My books *Toxic Nourishment* and *Damaged Bonds* open up some of these atmospheric conditions. Deprivation of emotional nutrients plays a big role in Winnicott's sense of psychic reality.

Therapeutic care is less an exorcism (as Fairbairn suggested, referring, in part, to exorcism of the internal saboteur, the self-attack system) than a holding of the lack or missing nutrients, a letting be and feeling one's way into what befell one, often involving recovery or discovery of basic agony, missing anger, and anger at what is missing. There are mixtures of agony, anger, grief, reparation, and a primary sense of creativity. Guntrip did seem to have the idea that he could somehow exorcise his loss—as if it could be found and healed. But he also realized something more pervasive and elusive was at stake, something that was part of the emotional air he breathed. That, in a way, he possessed two sets of lungs, simultaneously living or oscillating in two kinds of atmospheres, one fuller, one emptier. Perhaps a third as well, more malignant, attacking, overtly oppressive, obscuring emptiness. Guntrip realized that he was being disturbed by deadness, that there was something dead there to be disturbing, that this deadness was real. Yet he felt it was secondary to a primary lack in maternal care and should be fixable with proper care. He seemed to be satisfied that things fell into place. His vision of his life led to a kind of reconciliation, at-onement. But there is still much to learn, much to realize. Problems of profound emotional deprivation don't disappear with the wave of a psychoanalytic wand, but can be, in important ways, brought into a nexus of creative search and creative living. What I want to bring out is that Guntrip was sensitive to the fact that such problems exist, that they matter. For some people, perhaps many, problems such as those expressed by Guntrip remain invisible or indistinguishable from the flow of daily events, which they mark with dark spots that elude detection but have effects. The fact that someone like Guntrip can exist and take himself and his plight seriously is possibly part of an evolutionary growth of capacity to learn about our feelings, how they impact our lives even when the feeling of feeling is lacking. There is much to learn about how the sense of deadness impacts living. Perhaps there would be less violence in the world if more people could grapple with such difficulties. Perhaps more people will some day.

[After this interview, Eigen developed related themes in a new book, *Feeling Matters* (London: Karnac, 2007).]

Multiplicity, doubleness

Aner: One thread that runs through your writings is the double nature of human beings, its multiplicity.

Mike: We are not one thing. I think we have reached the point of being aware of multiplicity, pluralism in personalities and between personalities. Yet appearances can be deceiving. That a body appears does not mean a person experiences it. Some bodies are like hermit crab shells that inhabitants left behind. The problem of how we inhabit and personalize ourselves is important for psychoanalysis. There are people who are damaged beyond words, beyond affect. It is even possible for love–hate to be present with no one to experience it. Something of ghastly proportions happened. You can have a person without feelings and feelings without a person. I tried to describe conditions like this in *Toxic Nourishment* and *Damaged Bonds*.

I think of one man who gets along well in life. Success comes to him, and he has winning ways. He is a bit like individuals Winnicott describes. In his core, he does not feel alive, even though he is life-loving and active. His parents loved him but somehow he did not get through to them. They were absorbed in tasks, busy lives. His father taught him how to use his hands, make things. They were very efficient. Love and anger might have been there but somehow without impact or effect, as if there existed internal cotton padding, emotional sound-proofing.

These things are hard to pin down. How could he have such a good background and end up feeling so empty? Both parents focused on functioning, doing things well. Something in the quality of person-to-person, self-to-self emotional transmission was missing. Writers and therapists are sensitive to this kind of deficit. It is the kind of thing my parents would have shrugged off. It may be [that] society shrugs it off with violence and celebrity and top-dog economic madness. Perhaps we are afraid that if we pay attention to it the world will collapse. Or those who do not care about it will beat us.

Our awareness of doubleness or multiplicity of capacities is evolving. We have plasticity to be able to look at things one way, then another way. To live in Alaska or Hawaii, to work with our hands and our minds, to turn the other cheek, to turn things over and around. We think something and say, "Do I really mean that? Is that what I think?" And then something else comes, sometimes very different ideas, viewpoints. A similar plasticity goes on affectively: one feels more alive one moment, less alive another, then another state comes, and another. Many affective colourations pulse through a day.

Aner: It sounds like an amazing capacity of the human psyche.

Mike: It is an amazing capacity, this ability to take on lots of shapes and colours psychically, to identify and dis-identify with all manner of beings and events: aspects of animals, people, groups, happenings. Identifications with others, living or dead, in other times and places. When I was eighteen, I met Socrates, and the shock of truth forever changed me. My partial identification with Socrates changed my life. I don't feel worthy of such an identification, but I'm grateful for it. Many identifications and counter-identifications are part of our emotional–mental colouring. They may support us in living but they can undermine us too.

Sometimes we make fun of this plasticity; sometimes it is poignant or piteous. Woody Allen's movie, *Zelig*, for example, about a man who physically changes into a replica of the person he is with. Saul Bellow touches this when he describes Herzog's passivity in the face of relationships and life, particularly with stronger women whom he gives in to and leaves, adrift in waves of experience.

One of the best depictions of what I am getting at, celebrating, in awe of, is one I found in Nicholai Berdyaev in my twenties. He called it, or it was translated as, "neonic freedom". But I have never been able to find the reference. I read nearly everything of his in English. I don't know where I saw it but I know I did. He meant a kind of openness, a permanent neonate-like quality (Bion calls it embryonic) linked to freedom. Freedom to feel or think or be something else, something more. More human.

Sartre touches this when he describes human consciousness as a kind of nothingness, a radical plasticity unlike a hard and fast object. He went overboard, feeling we can create or re-create ourselves with virtual disregard of the history that weights our character. His threading neo-plasticity through choice ends up shrill: we can choose who we want to be; we can be what we want to be. A softer version might be to speak for a modicum of transcendence and that our input and responses matter. Writers have a right to push extremes. Sometimes they lose credibility in doing so. Sometimes the risk is worth it. Perhaps he became pan-choice in reaction to pan-determinism. Where he goes is not where I can or want to go. But I value his descriptions of the openness of consciousness, a certain psychic indeterminacy.

Freud touches an aspect of this capacity when he writes of the journey from dreaming to waking consciousness traversed each day. He suggests this as a basis for hope that psychosis is reversible, since he likens dreaming to a kind of transient psychosis.

We are kind of amphibian, ambidextrous, omnivorous psychically. We live in a plethora of experiential worlds collectively and individually. So much so, I sometimes get the impression that many species exist within our species, which is one reason communication can be so difficult. Plasticity is our bridge if we exercise it fully enough. Our interest in life, if not thwarted or stunted, will lead us to each other, no matter how foreign or strange we are. We are excited, not only threatened, by difference. We want to understand, not just conquer each other. We want to nourish and cultivate mutual permeability, creative vulnerability.

There is hunger for more and more dimensions of reality, whether we imagine, discover, or create them. This includes qualities of how we feel together and apart. Evolution—incessantly at work—involves a "neo-plasticity" that keeps us fresh.

Machines

Aner: Many believe that brain research would be able to answer these questions.

Mike: "And now class," says the professor, pointing to pictures on the screen, "here is how deadness works in this patient." Why not?

On the other hand, experience may get ahead of the brain; reach a thought or feeling that the brain has to catch up with. I think study and learning is good. Learn all you can about the brain. But don't reduce experiencing to what you can learn about the brain. I fear something like that is already in process. You have great new brain imaging machines and you start speaking of experience in terms of machine patterns. You *have* to reduce complexity, nuance, and fullness of experience to fit what your techniques allow you to talk about. Soon, a next step, is devaluing experiences the machine can't pick up or do justice to. A further step is saying such experiences don't really exist; they're artefacts of what you *can* explain, or *think* you can explain.

Aner: Can that happen?

Mike: It already has. The truncation of psychic reality to fit insurance payments or medication prescriptions, for example; or the impetus to denude the range of experience in order to fit definitions that those in power can manipulate, handle and use. There is a vicious movement in the United States by so-called empirical psychologists to render the psyche illegal, or, rather, throw suspicion on ways of working that lack "objective" evidence of "scientific" research. Such terms take on a pernicious slant, as the communicative field is narrowed to what a very aggressive group defines as "objective", "scientific", or outlaws as "subjective". Indeed, they raise the spectre of lawsuits against those who do not think their way (to me they sound a lot like right wing talk show hosts who bully and shout dissent or other viewpoints down). Just as psycho-analysis is achieving credentials as an independent profession in some states, a group arises that wants to outlaw it. You don't have to be overly paranoid to envision pressure groups lobbying to ban the psyche. A strong force is at work to constrict experience to fit reigning methods of influence. Perhaps it always has been so. But it seems to have picked up momentum, supported by better tech-nology and organizational, economic know-how. The secret, if it was a secret, is out: you can change the face of power by redefining reality to fit one's programme. The rapid dissemination of informa-tion and weaponry (winning lies, spins, slants, interpretations—not just physical weapons), coupled with public bullying and dimin-ished fear of cheating (self-interest as the greater good), are some factors that go into the burgeoning psychopathy we seem helpless to contain. At the same time, communication technology heightens consciousness of what happens as it is happening.

Another doubleness involves machines or our use or relation-ship to them.

Aner: In what sense?

Mike: I am thinking of machines—whether combustion or circuitry—somehow modelled after our bodies, especially the insides of our bodies. Old machines like cars or planes have heads and tails, something for vision, something to take in and get rid of, *à la* digestion. Cars make a funny anthropos, with visual head, rear intake–output, wheels (like a bug's or animal's legs) for locomotion. When I was a kid we'd learn that our nervous system worked like telephone networks. In graduate school, our brains became computers for a time. And so on. All these externalizations, possi-bly projections of our muscular and nervous systems in amalgam with respiratory, digestive, and sensory structures. There, outside of us, are our insides. We can partly read ourselves through our inven-tions. Sometimes they expand the way we see ourselves and some-times they reduce experience of ourselves. But they are not living tissue. They do not grow organically. They are not sentient. When we say they are sensitive we mean they function in fine ways. Machine sensitivity is a way of speaking. Most of us would not be ready to say that a machine is subject to the tragic agony and divine joy that erupts in art.

Aner: But machines also expand experience.

Mike: Of course. Some people, like Sherry Turkle, speak of spiritual aspects of our connection to computers. Machines not only increase production, they make certain kinds of linking activity possible across space and time. They can be enlivening. But they also play a role in deadening processes. We take in what we project. We begin to see ourselves in terms of our creations. We begin to think that living flesh and living mind function the way machines do. We begin to think we *are* machines. There is much evidence for this view. Amazing forms of surgery are made possible by it. Genetic miracles will be a medical resource. But what do machines feel? What is their emotional life like?

Psychoanalysis tells us that the emotional life of human beings is pretty messy. But we work with it. We grow with deformities that hold our pain, our trauma history. Ways we are misshapen are not just something that calls for surgery or mechanical repair. They are part of being a person. They result from personal pain. The sickness of our soul is part of individuality, something sacred, something holy. We are precious in our illness–wellness. We wouldn't build machines with as messy an emotional life as we have.

How many computers or cars have you had? How many marriages? For some people, the numbers are pretty close. But something in many of us balks at being disposable, substitutable, suitable for the dump or museum. Something in us says we are human—not just as lord, or master, or inflated superiority. Something heartfelt and caring is real. We want to do right by ourselves and each other. We want to help. A negative aspect of the machine model is that it deadens our need for help, human help, which is different from getting a larger capacity hard drive or speedier processor.

Aner: We treat ourselves like machines.

Mike: Because there are ways or attitudes in which we *are* machines, or, at least, treating ourselves or certain processes that way works. Machines grew out of our need for tools, to do things more efficiently, faster, better, cleaner. They work better for certain tasks than helping us live with our feelings. At the same time, I believe, we created machines in the hope of de-animating ourselves. Maybe making life more mechanical would solve what we came to call irrationality, emotionality, and untameable disturbance.

We can't blame machines for our de-animating tendencies. The latter antedated the mushrooming of machine-driven culture. We created gods in order to feel more alive. Or perhaps gods and machines arose together. Gods function as containers for deadness, projected attempts to transcend deadness. This can go haywire, more and more aliveness needed to counter a dead pull or undertow. You can't bring deadness to life no matter how much life you pour into it or aggravate yourself or stir yourself up. You have to go into the deadness, make room for it, and encompass it. We create myths to help us do that, then [we] deform our myths.

Many link increased momentum and spread of deadening processes with social atomization, industrialization, mechanization. Now we claim to be in a post-machine age, an information age. But business has become a kind of monster machine emphasizing economic efficiency. Efficiency feeding unending economic appetite, a devouring appetite eating lives and societies as it creates products and markets. The emotional x in the equation wreaks havoc. A power machine driven by determined, hungry egos.

And how do our brains work? Are they hard wired for destruction? For affection? For long-term bonds? For short-term excitement? For beauty? For rage?

Is the God centre close to the sex and anger centres? At least we have evolved to the point where we can ask questions of our brain. Even if we are programmed for destruction, we can address our chemistry and structure and have a say in what we do with it. We may, to some extent, even modify what our brain does, and can do so by what *we* do. I don't mean use of chemicals to modify brain chemistry, although that is a popular pursuit today. I mean, simply, the way we change ourselves by the way we address ourselves, by the way we use ourselves. We are given quite a mixture of capacities, quite a palette. Let's see what we can do with it. We have scarcely begun addressing, partnering, interacting with the challenge of our make-up. Yet, I believe, many of us try forays into this immensity over the course of our lives.

Aner: What would you say to your brain?

Mike: Let me speak to our brain now. Don't you, brain, remember many many years ago we almost accidentally got a glimpse of panoramic vision? Perhaps you played a role in giving us that glimpse, and we said to you, "Now, wouldn't it be great if we could really look around and have our own kind of aerial vision like the birds?" Our wish, our urgency, the way we used and wanted to use ourselves, pressured our organs to evolve. We didn't sprout wings but we stood up and raised our heads, turned our necks and looked around. We grew upright, achieved a vertical dimension. Saw better, yes, saw more in a glance. Panoramic vision has its uses but also gives us a thrill, a feeling of infinity, such marvellous vistas of sky, colour, expansive horizon. You, dear brain, developed structures coordinated with the rest of my body to support my impulse to be more, to experience more, to open heavens to my gaze, to open earth to my touch. You did that for me once, you can do even more now.

Just like you, our brain, evolved to thrill us with magnificent horizons, so can you go further to support our vision of getting along together, of respecting, tolerating, even cherishing each other, of going beyond war to solve difficulties and feel might. Some of us feel our oats and test our strength by solving problems, by working with form and colour, even by learning how *you* work. Some push their bodies to new limits in dance, in sport, in taste. And some— and more must do this—pit themselves against their emotional make-up, challenge their essence, their ways of being human. They pressure you to evolve, to go further, by going further themselves. Kant says a glimpse of ethical beauty is more breathtaking than the beauty of the starry skies. But how to achieve a working ethics, an incarnate caring respect? A prophetic vision with ancient roots—is it exerting more or less pressure now? Is it forcing or easing its way to new births, a new touch?

Meanwhile, it is dangerous to walk down a street in Brooklyn, New York, where I live. The journey from subway to home is a wrong kind of adventure. And the threat that runs through the world, not just of crime but terrorism. We are threatened from without and within, from high as well as low places.

I felt mugged by the presidential elections in the year 2000. The 2004 election is around the corner and I have not recovered from the last one. Election rape is what I felt. The disenfranchisement of sectors of voters, local and national bullying, capped by being run over by the highest court of the land. The smug grin at the top of the flagpole representing accretion and seizure of power. "Out-foxed", as the title of a documentary declares. Out-bulldozed is closer to the ground. What happened afterwards was worse, feeding economic mania on national and world griefs. Power suckled by trauma. A far cry from Kant's ethics. Corporate economic madness on the one hand, fundamentalist terrorist madness on the other: we are crunched between viral realities.

Aner: Keep talking to your brain, Mike.

Mike: But, brain, you gave us ethical sensation, sensitivity to mutuality, a sense of the infinite preciousness of every human being. And now that we have this precious sense, we want to find ways to use it well. Did you give it to us as a kind of social cement to balance the lust for power, to soften exercise of might? Do you tease us with love, a junior partner in the larger scheme of things? What say do we have in how we are structured and how our structures work? Should or can we pressure you towards democracy? What would that look like; do either of us know? Do we need to feed on so much hate?

You will have to find ways to support our forays, our challenges to ourselves, our need to care about what we do to each other. You will have to find ways to provide organismic support for our attempts to learn how to nourish better links between others and ourselves. We set this programme for ourselves. You will have to configure somatic backing for our needs and, at times, lead the way with somatic inspiration. You have been good at mixing beauty and goodness with trauma and horror. You have been good at sustaining social madness and lives devoted to discovery. But we need and want more. We are determined to try to do better. We will need much luck and help from each other and from you.

Or have we gone as far as we can? You can see this with dogs that ache to do more. Out of eager love they try to push just a little further, perhaps to please, perhaps for greater contact, they strain to go a little beyond what their equipment can support. They reach for something extra, and then fall back, a bit exhausted and disappointed that they could not quite break through the barrier, a neurological ceiling that brings experience to a standstill. It's as if a further stretch of consciousness is on the tip of its brain, but not quite, almost. And he falls back to being a normal dog.

Have we reached our ceiling? Will it be more of the same from here on in? Or will you respond to our pressure for more? Can you rise to our need to develop ourselves without destroying each other? Can we change to meet such a possibility, to create such a possibility?

Aner: It sounds utopian.

Mike: The prophetic vision of peace is utopian: lion and lamb nourishing each other, turning weapons into tools. The opposite of predator–prey, the food chain. It looks as if peace is opposed to nature. If this is so, it is a worthy opposition, struggling with ourselves, opposing ourselves as part of a path towards growth, a path towards peace. Peaceful opposition and struggle, peaceful war, this fight with ourselves. A funny kind of utopian war with human nature that grows from human nature into the future as far as we can see. Within the individual, within the family, between local and international groups. A welcome war, a war that makes us more fully humanly caring, more careful (care-full).

Aner: All Utopias have actually failed.

Mike: No one has solved what to do with our destructive elements, our destructive tendencies. Don't we need a certain amount of psychopathy to survive? A certain amount of lying, cheating, tricking is natural and unavoidable. We are not straight lines, clear-cut machines. We are creatures with a devilish side and the devil needs its due. But things can and do get out of hand. Psychopathy of everyday life builds, spreads, gains momentum. Soon lots of monsters are running around the social body, the family.

We are not a finished project. We are in process. We are not done. We are not going to undo our psychopathic element in the real, foreseeable future but we do not have to give up learning to work with it, turning it to good stead, to become better rather than worse psychopaths. By better, I mean turning psychopathy to good purpose, to humane purpose, a psychopathy with heart vs. heartless psychopathy.

Coetzee, the South African writer and winner of the Nobel Prize, talked about cosmetic morality. I think things in my country are a good deal more lethal than cosmetic. The stunning dominance of a political group that incites people to act against their own interest, to feed the economic superiority of a very few. A kind of psychopathic, manipulative, controlling morality, not just cosmetic. Acting as if they are doing the greatest good for the greatest number, while fleecing the nation. Teaching by example that winning pays, lying, cheating, bullying works.

Yet we are not only psychopathic. There is a heart-thread, a will to help, a need to do good by ourselves and others, to make life better for all, not just for ourselves. We do want to help each other. These streaks compete. But they can also feed each other, work together. We have to learn more about how different capacities can make things better and not thrive at the expense of other lives. We are predators and saints and much else. There are those who really believe it is worthwhile to help another person, to help for its own sake, and those who use ethics as an exploitative tool. In the Bible the ethical voice is a whisper within (although at Mount Sinai it was thunderous). A still, small voice that creates the greatest whirlwinds of all, a revolution of human nature, a lived ethics of sensitivity to self and other.

Psychosis

Aner: Can a psychotic experience lead to aliveness?

Mike: It can. It is fashionable to associate madness, trauma, and deadness. But psychotic states can be very alive, heightened states. They can change lives, depending on how things go. For some, they remain reference points, points of intense experiencing, in which much is learned about self and cosmos. Dimensions of being and experiencing open. Psychosis can be devastating, frightening, but also extremely meaningful. A tough balancing act, especially since there are many kinds of psychosis, from deadness, blankness to hyper-aliveness, and many combinations. many factors to take into account. For some, the best they can do is gain support to modulate it, make believe it isn't there, learn to respond to signals that things are going off, learn to manage it. But there are those who can do better.

Arieti speaks of psychotic individuals mourning loss of their psychosis as they get better. Loss of the heightened intensity, hyper-meaning. Loss or diminishing of states that can feel so fiercely, if frighteningly, creative. A lot of personality destruction goes into this creativity sensation, but there is much of value that takes time to sort out. There are, perhaps, few experiences that feel as total, even if this "totality of experiencing" runs through very narrow channels. This is true, too, of certain rage states, which feel absolutely total and consuming yet make use of a very narrow range of emotion and cognition.

Aner: Medication might relieve the psychotic symptoms but it can also destroy its meaningful aspect.

Mike: Today it is more the rule to tone down psychotic experiencing with medication. This helps many people but there is a price. It makes it more difficult to benefit from what one goes through, to begin assimilating, working with psychotic modes of experiencing. One tries to tone it down, shut it out, get rid of it, go back to business as usual. Much is lost in this process. I have heard many individuals who controlled or "got out of" their psychosis this way later complain that things are not as meaningful as they once were, nor as alive. Medication made it possible to live a life, a more normal life, but not as alive a life as they might have. For some, psychosis is a portal to heightened meaning and aliveness which, if sustained and worked with, informs a larger existence as time goes on.

We speak a lot about psychotic emptiness but also need to say more about psychotic fullness. To help individuals taste and work with twists and turns of psychotic emptiness and psychotic fullness is one thing: damage is confined to pockets of individuals, although personal cost is high. Unconscious addiction, attachment, hunger for psychotic fullness in the social body raises the stakes, since multitudes are caught in the web of mad needs which often pass as normal. Madness is rationalized as the way things are. Language jokes and philosophizes about it: we say life is crazy, the world is crazy, we are crazy. *And we are.* What can we do about it or with it? How do we absorb it?

Aner: This raises questions you address in *Emotional Storm* about our various ways of relating to suffering.

Mike: That agonizing experiencing can be meaningful and have varying outcomes is an important fact to reflect on. We dismiss it too quickly by referring to "masochism" or attachment to pain or conditioning. There is something about the need for total use of self, pushing experiencing past what can be experienced, "max-ing out" as they say. This need for intensity may play a role in maintaining terrible conditions in society as well as individual lives. It can be done in pleasurable ways like using one's equipment maximally and beyond the maximum in some way, perhaps drumming, dance, warfare, hunting, farming, or manufacturing, inventing, selling, buying, making greater and greater profits. But the same need to get the most out of one's equipment, to take it to the edge, its maximum, and still further, applies to the need for agony as well as pleasure. There are instances in which pleasure-seeking obscures a need for agony. Sometimes one gets inklings this is happening when pleasure leads the way to agony. Agony as a portal of illumination is one profile, as part of madness and trauma another, as a goal and by-product of power still another. We need to squeeze the most out of our experiential equipment and find ways to do it, personally, aesthetically, and socially, even—often especially—if it hurts.

A sense of national and international paralysis gets writ large in face of explosive cunning and perverse throbs of power. In the daily news we see portrayals of excruciating devastation punctuated by faces crazed with self-satisfaction. What will it take to expose our need for excruciating states, for devastation, and to work with this traumatic underpinning? To what extent do we inflict and undergo injury in order to be heroic?

Trauma feeds art and war. Madness feeds trauma. A lot of deformed creativeness goes into psychotic fullness. A lot of creativeness deals with deformations, including a sense of its own deformity, which partly drives it.

Aner: Perhaps your views about psychosis, especially that it is part of human condition, may explain the fact that most of your influences are European.

Mike: Yes, as I was cutting my psychoanalytic teeth, there was more interest in Europe in psychotic dynamics. I liked the idea that madness is part of the human condition. I found my way into psychotic elements of experience quite early, but there was very little in the New York analytic milieu to share this with. To give a flavour: my original title for *The Psychotic Core* was *Madness*. Not only did I have a hard time finding a publisher, the one that finally published it believed "madness" [to be] too pejorative and insisted on a title change. The word madness was common overseas. Winnicott used it as a matter of course. Perhaps one of the many ways psychoanalytic prudishness, up-tightness, stuffiness came out was fear of madness, keeping it at a distance, attempting to filter it through codified oedipal analysis and a rather ritualized version of structural theory.

Aner: *The Psychotic Core* brings out the centrality of psychosis in psychoanalysis.

Mike: It almost seemed like a hidden centrality that needed "outing". An important part of the conflict in the British Society between Anna Freudians and Melanie Kleinians had to do with how one related to psychotic dynamics. Focus on psychotic processes caused quite an upheaval, yet the enormous madness that marked human life, the World Wars, for example, the ghastly destruction, couldn't be ignored. One does not have to look far for varieties of madness in the world today.

In the first chapter of *The Psychotic Core*, I show how central the phenomenology of psychotic states is for the formal concepts Freud developed. His depictions of id, ego, superego contain elements of psychotic experience: id as cauldron of seething excitations out of contact with reality, common sense, and the law of contradiction; ego as hallucinatory organ developing anti-hallucinogenic properties; superego going haywire, substituting self-destructive moralistic judgements for genuine ethics. Freud's structural theory is a kind of implicit portrayal of psychotic states. In a sense, Freud uses concepts built up from psychotic elements to treat neurosis, suggesting how important psychotic dynamics are in neurotic organizations.

Freud writes that dreams are a kind of temporary madness giving hope to being able to treat psychosis proper more successfully. If the psyche can go in and out of psychosis and traverse an amazing range of states throughout day and night, what stops us from harnessing such plasticity in therapy? If mad states are "reversible" in daily life, why shouldn't psychosis be treatable? Freud explicitly traces madness in everyday life through transference phenomena: e.g., devotion to national leaders, religious authoritarianism, falling in love.

In *The Psychotic Core*, I organize psychotic processes in terms of hallucination, mindlessness, boundaries, hate, epistemology, and reversal. More areas could have been chosen, not less. I present double helixes in terms of the distinction–union of self–other and mind–body, and chart deformations along these various dimensions, functions, capacities, realities. As in all my books, I tried to let the thing itself speak in so far as I am able, in this case, to let psychosis speak. In fact, this book does speak to many people, especially those intimately acquainted with the domains opened up. I still get calls and e-mails from people helped by it and from seminar leaders who use it in teaching.

Madness is an intimate part of American literature. You would think American psychoanalysts would have gravitated towards it sooner. Maybe Freud's negative reaction to American psychoanalysis unconsciously had to do with the latter's too easy evasion of the tragic dimension, its descent into cant, or its conversion into a business, a money machine, rather than a calling, a vocation, a psychic lust. A double manic evasion: let's have fun and let's make money. Of course, Freud was motivated by making a living, but he also had the psychic hots. The psyche turned him on. Making a living was important, but so was psychic creativity. Psychoanalysis was not merely or mainly a business.

Freud recognized [that] America was not without its possibilities. He remarked that Americans might be crazy enough to be able to treat psychosis. This was not meant as a flattering remark, but there is a lot here to be unpacked. It looks as if Britain beat us to it, but some of us are catching up. So—who is madder? Austria was sane? Freud's relation to reality was spotty, too, witnessed by his certain death in a concentration camp (like his sisters) had he not been practically forced by outsiders to leave as the Nazi storm began to take its toll.

Ego–body boundaries

Aner: The I-feeling and the body feeling seem to have a special interest for you.

Mike: This is a phenomenon that vexed many workers, especially Federn and Milner. In *The Psychotic Core*, I muse how differently American psychoanalysis might have looked had Federn won over Hartmann. Hartmann has brilliant things to say about psychosis, but Federn's work is the living sea of it.

Federn was influenced by Husserl as well as Freud. He was especially interested in variable ego boundaries, e.g., the latter's expansion and contraction. Boundaries can so expand that the cosmos is felt to be part of the self and [the] self one with the cosmos. Boundaries can so contract that almost all life is foreign. In illness, for example, boundaries can shrink to exclude the body as not-me, enemy.

Federn observed that depersonalization—feeling unreal to oneself—often preceded psychotic breakdown. The I-feeling withdraws from world, from body. It even can vanish to itself. There are states in which I appears without significant body awareness. *I* variably expands and contracts to include or exclude the body. Winnicott, for example, tries to discover conditions that promote personalization of the body.

Koffka, in *Principles of Gestalt Psychology*, quotes a mountain climber's description of a dangerous fall, in which he is knocked unconscious. As he comes to, he sees a point of light outside him, then realizes that point is I, ego, himself. Consciousness gradually spreads and relocates him and his I in his body as body sense returns to awareness. In this instance, the one who is seeing is not yet an I. It takes a while to snap into shape and fuse with I sense *and* body sense.

Federn calls attention to ways I-feeling and body-feeling tease apart. For example, the many variations in being in or out of body as one wakes up or falls asleep. Psychotic states, too, show variations of being in and out of body. Federn found it difficult to subsume them under the notion of ego as first and foremost body ego. There are instances in which, as R. D. Laing emphasized, one leaves one's body because of threat. But Federn raises another possibility, equally important: one may be too threatened from nearly the beginning to enter the body in a real way. This latter more nearly fits Gnostic fantasy, the sense of soul or spirit in upper heaven, needing to be cajoled or induced to come down into the dank climes of embodiment and suffer earthly birth.

Federn, then, following Husserl, writes of the ego as first and foremost psychic ego feeling, a mental or transcendental or psychical I that expands to include body feelings. This more nearly fits important facts about psychosis. It can make a difference in clinical work whether one sees the self as leaving the body because of emotional threat and needing to reclaim lost ground, or whether the self must negotiate the body for the first time, so to speak. It is a problem of beginnings, facing dread of trauma that beginnings signify. It may seem a slight distinction, but there is a different yield.

Marion Milner spoke of consciousness going into the body from above or rising from within the body. Here you have a two-way movement, which gives the clinician latitude for creativeness, moving through, within or out of body and mind and self and psyche in all sorts of ways. I have tried to give some sense of clinical possibilities in *Coming Through the Whirlwind* and *Reshaping the Self*, with virtually verbatim sessions in each book. Even so, the ground to cover is much more than any of us manage.

Freud's remark that neurotics build castles, psychotics live in them, is a bare hint.

Aner: Freud portrayed the psychotic as withdrawing libido from objects and over-cathecting the ego, as in megalomania. Would you agree?

Mike: This has its uses. As the twentieth century unfolded, grimmer states were codified. It was not only a matter of an inflated I but of an I unreal to itself, an I that lost I-feeling. As if the I were not over-cathected but under-cathected, or, in Green's description, personality and ego suffer vast decathexis, a dying out of affect and realness, even and especially of self.

Bion comes closest, I feel, in describing the simultaneity of maximum and minimum emotion, too much and too little, Big Bang and null.

A lot hinges on the fate of affect in the therapy situation, affective fluctuations, connection–disconnection, from flooding to barrenness (suffocation–starvation). Federn already discovered that a positive transference—love of the analyst and the analyst's love of the patient—could help make the patient feel more real and the body and world more welcoming. Love invites the depersonalized soul into body and world. Of course, love is not enough, as affect stimulates fright and flight and fight and hardening, stiffening. Feeling, for the psychotic, often is associated with destruction, disaster. One is caught between alternate disasters: to feel or not to feel. One can see these states enacted in the political realm, where psychotic anxieties are psychopathically manipulated.

Society

Aner: You write a lot about destruction. You speak of the need to struggle with ourselves, what you just called the war of wars. Can you say more?

Mike: We are a very destructive group. We create many beautiful things. We look at the universe we are in and, by our standards, it is filled with destruction and beauty. Explosive processes, organisms devouring each other for sustenance; sunsets and sunrises exciting hope; moments of wonder and love. Freud simplified things by creating two main drives (made up of partial drives), but they are two of the central currents that have attracted religious thought, e.g., God's wrath and love or earlier imaginative dialectics of aliveness and death. We suspect our universe began with an explosion, a big bang. And we participate with our little bangs, which seem pretty big to us.

One terrific thing about psychoanalysis is its emphasis on working with destruction without being destructive. How does one work with destructive thoughts and urges without destroying? It's an open question. Far from solving it, psychoanalysis keeps opening it. For example, some people who have rages might notice that their rages scare their children and that the rages of their own parents scared them. They might connect with the fact that their tantrums make their children withdrawn or aggressive or anxious or just plain hurt. They may feel badly and fight to oppose their tendency to injure those close to them, and grieve over how they themselves were injured. However, some people simply do not catch on. They remain blind to themselves. Or, if they see, feel helpless to do anything about it. Destruction slips through. They may watch in impotent horror as their nature takes its toll on themselves and others.

In *Psychic Deadness* [Chapter Twelve, "Primary process and shock"—AG], I wrote about a patient who dated the moment he died to a dinner when his dad flew into a rage over something nonsensical. The boy numbed out and never regained full aliveness. One doesn't know how many times he may have died before, or partially died, or numbed or lost feeling. Or what went into being weakened over time, to the point that a supper rage tipped him over. We know his father was depressive and rageful. My patient, like a boxer sustaining body blows, must have taken pounding over years to the point of knock-out. To pin it on a particular supper is dramatic, but perhaps something like a screen memory. It provides a point to organize oneself around, a moment of death that stands for all deaths. It gives death a simplified history. A way to fortify oneself against the deaths to come. Often psychotic persons will imagine a time before breakdown as better. They feel if only they can get back to their pre-breakdown state, everything will be OK. They idealize the time before breakdown. As we go on, we learn [that] not everything was OK then, or ever. Disturbance plagued them ever since they can remember. The human race, too, has idealized times that never existed, a golden age, a utopian age, when in fact disturbance is part of the fabric of experience. My patient feels his life is damaged, yet he does not stop living it. There can be a lot of aliveness and good aliveness in a very damaged life.

Aner: Do you believe therapy can help society?

Mike: Therapy, after all, is a social product. It arose in a social context. Perhaps it is an attempt by society to inoculate itself against itself, an attempt at self-cure. Therapy is a response to atomization, mechanization, nationalism, the mushrooming commercialization of life on the one hand, and authoritarian influence on the other. It is the back and forth between persons that matters in therapy. One experiences the feel of the other, the feel of oneself. One is saying that there is value in intimate dialogue, investigation, exchange. The scale is small enough to feel oneself and the other. People need to feel themselves, to taste each other. It is a need in its own right.

We say the world is smaller than ever because of the technology that knits it together. But the world is also vaster. There are huge economic spaces, mobility, possibilities. Economics shift and masses of people are fired. Like geological shifts, earthquakes, storms, enormous thermal fluctuations, conditions change and more people are rich, more are poor.

Today, education is part of the mobility. It is still hard for me to get used to the idea that people go to school to do better financially. It is such an elemental fact. Yet college for me meant love of learning, worlds opening. It took me a long time to make the connection between education and making a living. Not because I was rich. On the contrary, I came, as you know, from a struggling, immigrant family. Strange, no? I think I was trying to carve a smaller world within the larger world, and pour myself into that. A world having to do with self, psyche, soul, spirit, experience. As I grew older, I connected more with the larger world around me, world in general. It took a long time for that spread to occur.

Therapy values a smaller space, a space you can pour yourself into. A human space to establish and explore relationship, connection. A place for feeling to evolve. People need to taste themselves, to chew on, digest each other. For some, therapy is a temporary support. They want to gather themselves and move on. For some, it is a way of life, a life-long process. Most are somewhere in between. One would like to think of therapy as a tool or method but it is more. It is not like an X-ray machine or surgical operation. It is part of the fabric of who one is, the fabric of meaning, the feel of life, one's own life. We are not talking about particular organs. We are engaging how we approach living, how we interact with life.

There are many cultural experiments creating smaller contexts for people to experience themselves, to counter feeling lost in a larger world that doesn't care, where everyone competes against everyone else. There is a personal sense in which smaller is better. I think, too, it is no accident that psychoanalysis grew up with great wars as background and horizon, providing a safe harbour [in which] to speak the unspeakable.

The question of whether therapy can help social madness is something I weep over.

Aner: That sounds very optimistic

Mike: I am not stupidly optimistic. But if I have a say as to whether to ally myself with a cynical undertow or with a caring heart, it is the latter I give a little extra to. Therapy has a hard enough time helping itself and helping people that come its way. To spread into a larger world is a tall order. It has happened already, to some extent. Various forms of therapeutic discourse are part of culture.

But dare we think we know how to help society? Are we developed enough, well enough to have beneficent impacts? We are a pretentious, contentious lot. Mental health "experts" are something to worry about. "Doctor, heal thyself" is always a good starting point. Nevertheless, we see how inextricably connected individual and social life are. Healing at any level works on others. Difficulties are so immense that little improvements may go unnoticed. On a one-to-one basis, a little goes a long way. On a larger scale, a little may seem *very* little, readily swallowed by callous structures and conditions.

The fact that we psychotherapists are a pesky, nasty bunch, like everyone else, does not mean we should shut up. Others don't, why should we? We are obligated to have our say, warts and all. We should have our say because no one will say exactly what we will. We need to make what contribution we can, however defective. If we wait until we are better, we may never be ready to help. Bion said he wrote, not because his writings were what he hoped for, but because if he didn't someone or something worse would fill the space.

Aner: How would you change society?

Mike: Like everyone, I have visions. Imagine pouring some fraction of the money that goes to military and corporate tax breaks into food, education and vocational programmes for the needy, sports and cultural participation programmes for those desperate to exercise themselves in less self-destructive ways. Like massive doses of penicillin for society. Community health programmes and developmental researchers helping mothers and babies and families interact better are a drop in the bucket, but a potentially important drop for those involved. I used to picture screaming booths scattered throughout the city, places people can go to safely scream. Now I picture someone to talk to, talking booths on city streets.

The gap between rural and city thinking is enormous. Mental health workers are concentrated in cities. We can learn a little from fundamentalist outreach groups and develop volunteer programmes to encourage interactive awareness. This would take enlightened government funding. Interpersonal disasters hit the news with people saying, "He was always crazy", or "so quiet", or "always a troublemaker", or "We had no idea anything was wrong". So often there is a disconnection between communication patterns in upbringing and difficulties in adolescence and young adulthood. As much as possible gets bypassed as normal or accepted as odd, without a working sense that help might be helpful. One hopes growing up will just happen and things will work themselves out. Even distributing movies portraying various interactive styles might touch some families.

We juggle blends of psychopathy and ethical sensitivity, jugglers going for the jugular, polar currents feeding creativity. As therapists, we spend a lot of time getting the feel of feeling. Do those jockeying for worldly power appreciate our keeping a space open for personal communication or do they scorn such needs? Can attempts at learning how to make contact with ourselves and each other make a wider difference? Is therapy part of a larger shift of attitude involving how we approach each other, a shift with a long path to travel? The longing to help continues amidst strife-born disasters. We hope it grows into something more than clean-up efforts following self-inflicted injury. We *can* have positive impact on our lives. Will what we learn with a few help many? Utopian thinking or effective faith?

Encounters: Bion, Green, Winnicott

Aner: Tell me about your encounter with Bion.

Mike: He told me to get married. I saw him when he was in New York City in 1978, giving seminars sponsored by a local psychoanalytic institute. He reassured me that marriage was not what I thought it was, not something to be so afraid of. He said, "It's just two people speaking truth to one another, a relationship to help mitigate the severity to yourself."

Aner: Did you bring up the marriage subject?

Mike: No, he brought that up. I did not raise the subject (laughs).

Aner: I wonder why he did that.

Mike: I am happy he did. I am happy someone woke me up, presented it in a way that I could hear, in a way that got through to me. Years later I saw in his Brazilian clinical seminars that he was a spokesman for the couple as biological unit. The reality of the couple played an important role in his sense of life. Nevertheless, remarks he makes in his seminars indicate awareness that coupling was not possible for everyone, that some people could not tolerate or manage it, that some would not choose it. For some, the damage or fear of damage was too great. I think he was addressing a fear of damage, telling me marriage was not only do-able, it would do me good. His "intervention" drew on a substantive background in his own life, his own history. I took it very seriously. I was in my forties, beginning to wonder if not now, when? He also told me to stop my analysis: "Stop analysis and get married."

Aner: Bion told you to stop analysis?

Mike: Yes, he told me that's enough. I'm not sure about his exact words but he conveyed a sense that I had enough analysis and there was more to get from living. Not that I wasn't living, but there was more. Maybe he thought I was too old not to be married. Maybe he thought I was overdue and needed a push. Maybe he thought I was substituting analysis for an important part of life, using analysis as a defence against a fuller self. He pushed me into birthing myself some more.

Aner: What more did Bion tell you?

Mike: He went on to talk about himself and his analysis with Rickman. I wondered why he spoke as much about himself as he did but I enjoyed the exchange. I felt he was sharing part of his life with me, sharing a bit of life together. Now I also see that bringing up Rickman fitted the theme of contextualizing analysis, of placing analysis within a larger horizon, a part of life but only a part. I think he was always pointing to the more of life.

He saw Klein after Rickman and, while his time with Klein gave him much to chew on, his time with Rickman supported a certain independence. There are trends in human nature that place us in danger. Transference is enriching but also potentially enslaving. I think he was saying that the independence Rickman supported acted as a kind of bulwark against being too fully assimilated by

Klein's analysis. There is something outside the system, something other, something more.

I see an overlap between what he told me about himself and his urging me to go beyond my current life. As if saying, don't be a slave to analysis and your current life, there's more, you can do and be more, you don't have to be confined by your present mode of being, there are other possibilities. Marriage was one possibility, scary and new. For a long time, I feared it would be too limiting. But I was at a point where not going on to it was even more limiting. Having affairs has good points but is not the same as life that opens through coupling, through family, the mystery of fecundity and profound emotional exchange.

In fact, I wanted to have a family from a young age, but got derailed by analysis in my twenties and thirties. I think my analyst must have feared he [had] created a monster by advocating postponement until the analysis was finished or farther along. Postponement never stopped and before I knew it I was in my forties. I had a budding career, but my desire for family suffered repression. Bion ushered in the return of a possibility. The thought of marriage made me feel more connected with myself and my long postponement was ending while there was time. Although I was in my forties, I did feel he was speaking as an older to a younger man, trying to help me into life.

Another thing he told me: dreams are real. He was sensitive to the realness of dreams. I long felt that, too. It was important to meet someone outside my world who felt that and meant it.

Aner: Dreams are real?

Mike: Maybe you have a scary dream and you say it's not really real. Maybe you don't know how to take it seriously. The dream expresses a frightening force and you try to dismiss it, play it down, make light of it. But Bion felt that dream reality really *is* real, emotional reality is real and ought to be related to in a seriously caring way. One needs to care about the dream. You dream of an attacker, an animal, someone you reject or who rejects you, nightmarish dreads, overpowering figures, erotic promise. Emotional possibilities that scar or feed a life.

A gestalt therapist years ago, Fritz Perls, would begin sessions having you say, "This dream is my reality". Or, "This dream is my existence". Perls would have you give voice to different objects in a dream, give expression to emotional realities [that] various aspects of a dream connect with. Freud used to say that we dream about things that would be destructive to enact while awake. He felt a reason we could have dreams was because of the safety sleep afforded: our bodies are out of play and helpless as our minds take off. Unfortunately, this notion of safety is a wish-fulfilment. Dream reality and outside reality interpenetrate, destruction in one feeding destruction in the other. We are the same being awake and asleep. Nightmares of inner reality are more than matched by those of outer reality and vice versa. Terror, fright, horror are not confined by sleep or waking. In an old formula, what is outside is inside and vice versa. To amplify Freud's suggestion, adults do what babies dream. More: grown-ups unleash dreads and furies babies can't imagine. Emotions of nightmares set the scene for adult horrors. You create situations in which states you dream about become real.

Elusive as dreams are, they help focus bits of emotional reality, often catastrophic impacts that require work. Dreams are part of a challenge. They are snapshots of intense emotional states that exercise us and need processing. They are part of our emotional digestive system. It is too simple to say that what does not get processed gets acted out. We do not know all the ins and outs of the links between feeling and action. But we can't ignore the realness of what dreams convey and get away with it for long. You unleash terrors and furies as an adult that you were helpless in face of as a child.

Aner: So he really shared with you thoughts about his life, his thinking . . .

Mike: Somewhat. He still was formal, somewhat stiff, measured, yet friendly, forthcoming, welcoming. Not in that easygoing, informal American way. He had a professional aura. But you felt he was tuned in, listening to something—a psychic bearing. That is, his formality and stiffness was not simply social manners but a kind of psychic sentience. A bird has a sort of stiffness, but it is alert and sensing.

He was alert to nurturing difference. At the time I saw him, I was running into trouble with a supervisor I respected and had been on good terms with. My supervisor began turning on me in harsh, uncalled for ways. He was helpful in the beginning, but as I came into my own and started publishing, he attacked. It was hard for me to come to grips with the fact that my development threatened him, that he was jealous of my success. It was hard for me to tear away and acknowledge this loss.

Bion talked about the difficulties of being different, having another sense of reality. How growth involves turbulence, not fitting in. I got the sense—it was gut, immediate—that he was speaking from his own experience. He spoke of "the nasty business of finding oneself" in a challenging but encouraging way. When I told him my dreams, he supported emotionally charged figures that challenged my frame, that touched my fears, turbulence figures. I threatened my supervisor the way a dream figure threatened me. Bion supported affective tumult *vis à vis* the inner or outer establishment. He supported movement, possibility, frame-stretching elements. Maybe this process involves becoming less phobic about emotional life (if that is possible), or at least realizing how frightened one is of aliveness. That aliveness frightens us may not be something we get over.

Aner: Tell me about your encounters with André Green.

Mike: About a year later I attended André Green's seminars in New York City and saw him for a session. This must have been in 1979 or 1980. In 1975, I saw Green speak at the International meeting in London. I used to go to many meetings in those days. This particular one had some special significance. Green was one of two lead speakers, the other was Leo Rangell, who I think spoke first. As the latter read, I thought, "This is dead, superego stuff, dead skin." When I mentioned him to Marion Milner a few days later, she said "He probably got there by working hard." When I exchanged words with Rangell he was nice to me, and I liked him.

When Green spoke I came alive and got interested. He read a terrific paper, "The analyst, symbolization and absence in the analytic setting (on changes in analytic practice and analytic experience)", published in the *International Journal of Psycho-Analysis*, 56:1–22. I felt: psychoanalytic imagination is alive. Green mediated psychoanalytic imagination and Rangell psychoanalytic deadness. I was thirty-nine and not too charitable. Two years earlier, my first papers in the *IJPA* began to appear. I was harsh in my judgements but felt I was gravitating to more creative currents of the field. The

1975 meeting was packed with creative sparks: I met Erik Erickson, Masud Khan, Donald Meltzer, and visited Marion Milner at her home.

A lot was going on I didn't know about. Only later I realized why Meltzer was bustling about. It had to do with Bion in Los Angeles and the scandal that a past president of the British Society fails to get full recognition in the Los Angeles Society. Bion's work with Los Angeles students would not be credited by the society there. This confirmed my sense that there was a war in psychoanalysis between forces of life and death, creativeness and stultification. Here was immediate, local dramatization of tensions Bion depicts between messiah/genius and establishment, tendencies in personality and society (*Attention and Interpretation*, 1970).

Rangell was spokesperson for the structural theory in a kind of codified way. Its application in New York was deadening in both ego psychology and classical forms. I well appreciate Lacan's railing against them. Tensions heightened, and finally Ana Freud took the stage, an old lady now. Many thought she'd support Rangell. He was in her camp. I don't think too many were prepared for what she said, but I was delighted. She took the mike and said, "The structural theory, the structural theory—we lived a long time without it." She was on the side of psychoanalytic aliveness. I smiled. There was room in psychoanalysis for imagination, for life.

So this is the background for my meeting with Green in New York. I studied his 1975 paper avidly and learned a lot. Not exactly new for me but he put it together clearly and firmly, a kind of manifesto, psychosis coming out of the psychoanalytic closet. Ways that neurosis/perversion helped organize psychotic anxieties. The writers I most gravitated to were interested in psychotic dynamics, Winnicott, Bion, and Klein. Of course, I read Sullivan and Searles, but I was drawn to the British and, later, the French. Green drew on Winnicott, Bion, and Lacan, as I did. I felt these three probably were the most creative psychoanalytic writers of the moment. Bion and Lacan were still alive. Winnicott had recently died. His drawings were exhibited at the meeting.

Green's description of double anxieties (e.g., abandonment–intrusion anxieties organized by acting out, splitting, somatization, decathexis) resonated with my sense of things, so much so, that as I read him I felt he must have read my work. So much of what was implicit in my work (my writings on time, for example) was explicitly elaborated in his papers.

I knew my suspicion that he was pilfering my stuff was nutty, but let it all hang out. I walked into our session and attacked him for stealing my material. I'm not sure what he felt but he didn't seem defensive. I went on to tell him more about my life, my current situation, my meeting with Bion, what the latter said about stopping analysis and getting married. He seemed to feel Bion had a point. Was I trying to get from authorities (Bion, Green) something I needed to do for myself? I told him about a dream about a woman that I was seeing. In the dream the woman was lovely, but there was something wrong with her eyes. I interpreted that this woman lacks something with regard to consciousness. Green, on the other hand, attempted to protect the "object" from my destructiveness. He said something along the lines: "It's your dream and your aggression created this image, marring her, seeing her in a negative light." I was finding defects to dismiss her, finding excuses not to have to be with her. Maybe something was wrong with *my* eyes: seeing faults to justify fleeing. Green protected the object from my attacks. I knew immediately what he was doing. Saw it, felt it. I came in attacking Green and he survived it. And in my dream I turned a woman I was interested in into someone to negate, spoiling a potential mate. He sided with the object relation, increasing awareness of my destroying objects I was involved with. It took me another thirty sessions with yet another therapist and a year or two later I got married. Three therapists teamed up (British, French, and American) to finally get me across the line. It took a lot to link up with myself and do what I long felt I wanted.

Aner: Green must have said it in a very empathic way. Interpretations that defend the object and not the self can sound judgemental.

Mike: He was not attacking. He was firm. He was clear and he had a theory and knew what he was doing, a bias towards the object relation. To me it didn't sound judgemental because it affirmed a tie with life.

I've spent a lot of time going over my trauma history. Still do, more deeply and fully than ever. I could turn the dream into analysis of a bad object. Green saved the dream from me, from a destructive way of seeing. He protected my psyche from me. He did it deftly, firmly, light of touch, clearly. He was protecting a link with life from attacks on it. I found his remark supportive, in that attacks on linking did not have the last word. The object—Green, my wife-to-be, my psyche—survived my attacking aspect. A kind of use of object (Winnicott) situation: the other surviving destruction becomes more fully other, someone one can be with. At the same time, you put a tracer on your destructive tendency, modulate it, and use it more creatively. It takes a lot of work to live with someone. As Freud pointed out, it is not clear whether or not destruction will have the last word—will we as a human group destroy or degrade ourselves beyond recognition? To withstand, forestall, divert, avert, or modify destructive tendencies in our personal lives—this is part of what we must work with. And in this particular instance, Green did so very well.

Aner: Did Green ever answer your charge of plagiarism? Did he give you a good reason why your papers looked similar? Maybe you wanted him to admit his plagiarism and apologize.

Mike: In my inner being I wanted him to sustain the situation. I did not want him to collapse, go dead, retaliate, or get over-analytical under attack. I wanted something else to happen. On the other hand (laughs), I would have loved an apology. I would have loved him to say, "You know, Dr Eigen, all the best things I've done I've gotten from you" (laughs loudly). But I knew it wasn't true. I didn't write the many papers he wrote before I started publishing. Some of the things he did were in the air. His dead mother paper, for example. Talk of the dead mother and toxic introjects were part of the New York milieu long before either he or I were writing. In spite of differences, we do breathe the same psychoanalytic air. But he could not resist saying near our session's end, "You know, the ideas you think I took from you—the English translations of my papers came out much later than the originals I wrote in French." I smiled. I forgave him for that. It made him more human. If the situation were reversed, I doubt I could have held it back either. But I was glad he held it back as long as he did. He showed me what an analyst can do and added to my appreciation of the power of analytical experience, not necessarily "classical" analytical experience. I know so many people who were victimized by classical analysis and loss of affect. Here was an affirmation of affect in a profound sense both on Bion's part and on Green's part.

Aner: Tell me about your encounter with Winnicott.

Mike: I saw him one time for several hours in 1968 right before he came to United States. I was passing through London after a trip to Israel and was in graduate school working on my PhD. I walk in and he greets me: "Hello, Dr Eigen, I am sorry I haven't read your work." I tell him I am just a student and that I haven't written anything. He treated me like a king. It was beautiful. He had this grace. He looked a little like an old woman. I thought about Jung's remark about how sometimes when one ages one takes the characteristics of the opposite sex. Women become more masculine and men more feminine. I don't know what he was like when he was younger but he did look a kind of wise, old woman.

Aner: Why did you come to see him?

Mike: I came to see him because I was a younger man and thought that would be a nice thing to do, to enrich my experience.

Aner: Was it also for personal consultation?

Mike: No. This one was not for personal consultation. At that time I was near a dramatic end of eight years of analysis. It didn't occur to me to have sessions with Winnicott. I wanted the exposure to a rich and creative man, to see what it felt like.

Aner: What did you talk about with Winnicott?

Mike: He did a lot of talking and I listened. He was a wonderful mixture of modesty, humility, and grace. He had his own particular way of being absorbed in his own reality and his own thought. He asked me why I wanted to see him and not R. D. Laing. Why did I call *him*? He said everybody wanted to see Laing. Well, I actually called Laing too, but he was too busy to see me (laughs). He started talking to me about Laing. Apparently the British like to gossip, psychoanalytic gossip. They spill the beans about each other. Americans take their personas more seriously, more prudish about professional image, more investment in creating the way they want to be seen. Being too personal might wreck the image—what will your colleagues say, God forbid. It is a funny prudishness in

American informality. Maybe there's fear of lawsuits (promiscuous suits related to prudishness? emotional starvation filling itself with money?). Bion understood how dangerous it could be to reveal oneself and one's work. He spoke about real work looking messy to the outside world. Analysis can look strange and irresponsible and mad to the outside, even to other analysts. Perhaps we've reached the point where it's not sex that scares people about psychoanalysis, but madness.

Aner: What did Winnicott say about R. D. Laing?

Mike: Winnicott was good enough not to say anything about how much Laing took from him. He said he was worried about Laing losing his grip on clinical practice. Laing was a star and doing star things. He might not have the desire, endurance, or persistence to sit with patients. Years later I discovered Winnicott's fears were justified. Some of Laing's patients consulted me and reported he was into working with them during LSD episodes, then lost interest and handed them to someone else for longer-term work. He lacked patience or interest for "working through". He was into the excitement of rapid opening, quick intense hits. A couple of these people reported intense peaks on LSD, but feeling dead afterwards, dead in most of their life. They were seeking help for deadness.

Perhaps the centre of my meeting with Winnicott occurred when he got up from his chair by his desk without warning (where he served the two of us sherry), walked across the room, screwed himself up in a kind of intense corkscrew at the end of his couch, twisted around, fell into a state of intense concentration, then said, "Here, maybe this will convey a sense of it," then went on to tell about a woman in analysis who needed him to sit still behind her as she centred his face in her hand-held mirror. He saw that his face was off-centre and moved to "help" her centre it. He immediately realized his error.

"If you had done that six months ago, I'd be back in hospital," his patient said. He knew she was right. In trying to help her get it right, he was like her mother, unable to tolerate not being the perfect centre of her mind. I was left with a sense of the importance of learning to tolerate being off balance, off kilter, off centre. Even being dangled and tantalized by another without loss of patience, faith, and skill. There is so much in psychoanalysis that pressures the analyst to precociously tie things up, bring things to premature closure, to stay on top of what can be a precarious, vertiginous situation. The analyst must work to ready himself to be different from the one-sided, duplicitous stance bullying politicians too often present.

But there are psychoanalytic bullies too. Winnicott kept asking me whether he should accept an invitation to speak in New York, would he be welcome, would people want to hear what he has to say. I was perplexed. He was asking me, a graduate psychology student, about how the New York Psychoanalytic Society would respond to him. A Society that trained psychologists only on condition [that] they sign a form pledging to use the training for research, not practice. Only medical doctors were fit to practise psychoanalysis. What did I know? What could I say? I was baffled. How did the big boys play?

Aner: What was your answer?

Mike: All I could say was that I and people like me or with similar interests would love to hear him speak, but I couldn't vouch for the establishment. So much was happening at that time, 1968: student ferment, protests, glimpses of a different world. Soon cracks in the medical stranglehold on psychoanalysis would widen, breakthroughs of psychoanalytic imagination were already on the way. But the time was not yet ripe for Winnicott. It was ripening, but would take several waves.

Winnicott got slaughtered. He presented his "use of object" paper at the New York Psychoanalytic Society, was butchered, went to his hotel room and had a heart attack.

Aner: Fifteen years later you published the first serious study of his "use of object" writing, in a paper entitled, "The area of faith in Winnicott, Bion and Lacan", and soon after received a letter from his wife, Clare Winnicott. Let me quote some of it:

> I must say how delighted and relieved I was to find that at last someone had really understood the "Use of an Object" paper, and seen it as an idea that revitalizes basic living and gives it another dimension. I know that for Donald this was the climax of his theoretical formulations—the place that he had been seeking to arrive at, and I think this can be seen in his previous work as one thing

led to another. The "Use of an Object" paper was in a sense his final word, his resting place . . . I remember one summer Sunday evening when Donald read the "Object" paper which he had been working on all day and had just finished—he read it to me for the first time after dinner. My response was total, and I knew that he had said something complete for himself which he had been working up to all his life. He had also said something about *us* and the way we lived. A momentous evening.

Mike: He gave this paper in New York and was cut down without defending himself. Perhaps he sought to create a use of object paradigm, sustaining attack without retaliation. Perhaps he felt the reality he sought to convey was beyond the resources, as yet, of the attackers. Clare Winnicott remained bitter about this event and felt some measure of redemption when the first explication of Winnicott's fertile concept, the first paper calling the analytic world's attention to it, came from New York. For years I received letters from people touched by the Winnicotts in London, saying how glad they were to have a good object in New York.

Trauma

Aner: In your companion books, *Toxic Nourishment* and *Damaged Bonds,* you seem to be saying that psychological damage is an intrinsic part of every meaningful dyad.

Mike: Is that such a novel idea? It doesn't seem new to me. It does need to be understood more deeply and made part of the public domain in useable ways. Damage is part of life processes generally, part of the way life works. Damage is part of physical processes. Everyone gets more or less damaged at birth. Infants get brain damaged, to some extent, through the birth process. Birth processes are damaging. A certain degree of damage is normal. We don't live in a damage-free world. But I didn't begin my career as a psychologist thinking this way. I used to think distinction between health and illness was clearer. Psychologists I read distinguished between growth processes and destructive processes, e.g., Erich Fromm's writings on productive love and work vs. escapist, authoritarian tendencies, or emphasis on conflicts between forward and backward movement, autonomy vs. arrested development. I gained a lot from such readings at the time, but life has taken me elsewhere, further. One can make such distinctions in an idealized, conceptual way. But reality is something else.

As I got deeper into work with patients and myself, concepts of damage and health began to meld. Perhaps it was my patient population or me, but one reaches places where, so to speak, injured and healthy tissue becomes indistinguishable. The love that nourishes is also the love that damages. For many individuals, the bonds that sustain them and make life possible are bonds that maim them and make life impossible.

Aner: But that's a very unusual view in psychoanalysis. Doesn't Winnicott, for example, mean that if there is a good enough bond between mother and infant, a good primary maternal preoccupation, there should not be any sustained damage?

Mike: I don't know if that is a Winnicottian view. Winnicott is not a simple theorist. He is a multi-faceted theorist. I doubt if good mothering precludes damaging processes. Maybe "good mothering" helps mitigate them, find a way through them, and even face them. Perhaps an element of good mothering provides some working ability to help come through traumatizing tendencies. Speaking about these things satisfactorily is difficult. Work with certain people finds itself concerned with attachment to a bad object that provides sustenance, a kind of death-bringer that signifies life. Add to that a kind of innate self-traumatizing tendency that traumatizing objects intensify—our work is very challenging.

But one does not have to do this in terms of bad or good. For example, Bion writes, "When two personalities meet, an emotional storm is created". This is in one of his last essays, "Making the best of a bad job". It is a sentence I love and made the basis of a book, *Emotional Storm*. For those who can tune in, our impacts on each other are varied, nuanced, mixed, a kind of emotional storm made up of many elements, like a rainbow made up of many colours. I get the urge to coin a term, *primary emotional storm*. Emotional responsiveness is normal. It is part of being alive, human. What Bion points out, one or another way, is that we do not know what to do with it. We think and feel without ability to digest what we think and feel. Our capacity for production is ahead of our capacity for assimilation in many spheres.

Part of the problem is evolutionary. We need to evolve more of a psychic digestive system. As I've often said, we live, more or less, in a state of psychic indigestion. This wreaks havoc in the larger social, political, economic spheres. It wreaks havoc in individual lives as well. Artists and writers are parts of long-term cultural digestive processes. And I suspect disciplines like yoga and meditation and certain forms of prayer are partial attempts at this too. The depth psychologies are giving it a try in their ways, part of a pattern of discovery and digestion.

Freud spoke of flooding as primal trauma. This overlaps with Bion's sense of primal emotional storm. Freud's depiction of psychological and neurological life share certain structures. For example, cortical mechanisms of inhibition and selection work with and against sub-cortical pushes, drives, and arousal. It is pressing a more discretionary I. Such binary pictures are fine, but the emotional fields, the emotional swirls and welling that experience opens, lose something by yielding too quickly to binary organizations.

The ever unassimilated more of experience is part of what eggs us on. It is part of what keeps life fresh. We try to regulate the more, the flood of events, the emotional flood. Our mechanisms for doing this often work against us. We dampen the sound of ourselves too much and become tone-deaf to feelings. We become too rigid or splatter, explode, disperse, thin out. We need to cultivate our psychic palette and learn to mix and temper emotional possibilities. Not just pharmaceutical cocktails—affective cocktails! I fear precocious over-reliance on medication will damage our plasticity.

Aner: The Bible is often mentioned in your writings in the context of emotional storm.

Mike: I often see the Bible as a kind of protracted emotional storm, storms within storms, an emotional storm over time. The great flood, of course. But flooding doesn't stop or start with the Noah's Ark story. Freud called God a volcano god. Fire, thunder, sparks, might, energy, more id than superego. We are taught that id–superego are tight partners. Their story is a story of struggle and conflict on many levels. No wonder peace and a day of rest are so valued.

One thread, one way of viewing the storm: the Bible expresses what it feels like to be a baby, the fate of goodness and good feeling in a world of trauma. It is a world where pleasure and pain commingle, where agony hits out of the blue, where one's whole personality is shaken by confusing events beyond control, repeatedly shaken. One is shaken and reforms in better or worse ways all life long.

One way of reading the Bible code: it gives political, mythic, poetic expression to what it feels like to have feelings: love, passion, attachment, betrayal, murder—currents criss-crossing in narrative form.

Aner: For you the Bible is a big stew of emotionality, a big splash of emotions that appear this way and that.

Mike: Call it primary emotionality, primary splash (laughs)—traumatizing, uplifting, crashing. When we say God is exalted we sense we also are speaking of emotional exaltation as such. The way feelings rise and fall and splish-splosh. The Bible is filled with ethical curses, disobedience, just and unjust authority, generative–destructive impulse, law that saves and kills. There are also pressures that elude narrative, personality pressures that no official story or doctrine define. The pressure that personality is, [the] pressure being exerts on itself. We are ever outside the net of our stories, no matter how trapped by them we are.

The Bible mentions a remnant, a still small voice, good seeds, a faith thread that comes through the storms. There is a struggle between faith (in life, in goodness) and other tendencies.

Aner: The same struggle that appears in Winnicott.

Mike: Winnicott tries his hand at explicating and expressing a voice of this faith thread, in his transitional experiencing and object usage portrayals. He tries to do justice to the freshness of self, otherness, emotional interweaving. In doing this, he breaks new ground. In his portrayals, human experience evolves. When psychoanalysis is at its best, we participate in the evolution of personal experience. And in parts of Winnicott's writings, the feel of human life itself opens some more.

Aner: In a complementary formulation, Winnicott speaks of trauma hitting as personality begins to form.

Mike: A hit rocks with emotional waves through the Bible, through Shakespeare, through Nietzsche, through Rilke and, of course, through Freud, the volcano god's fire. Hysterical, paranoid streaks mixed with love of life embedded in destructive tendencies. Trauma is being inflicted on us, elaborated through the psychic touch of others. Winnicott calls the traumatizing–traumatized psyche what it is: mad. The mad hit, the mad black winter, the mad deformation, the mad quest. Madness X, agony X. Is it an accident that a recurrently appearing psychotic patient in Bion's writings is called X?

Bion and Winnicott have more in common than is ordinarily recognized. Winnicott, too, is concerned with a certain insufficiency in face of emotional life and intensity of experience, particularly related to catastrophic impact. In one formulation, published in 1973, "Fear of breakdown", he depicts an infant at the mercy of emotional storms and primitive agonies it lacks ability to process or even undergo. Raw affect fields uplift, dash down, overwhelm, decimate. He described emotions in a threatening, menacing mode, emotions as devastating, beyond bearing. I think the plagues and locusts and famines of the Bible refer to emotional as well as physical facts.

Winnicott writes that fear of breakdown often refers to breakdown that happened early in life but remains unprocessed or unacknowledged. He puts a somewhat positive cast on it by saying that over time we develop capacity to work with states that were once too much for us.

Aner: But he is also saying that the sense of breakdown never leaves us.

Mike: Part of our underlying anxiety is fear of not being up to the states we undergo.

We break down in smaller ways throughout the day. Now we are more together, now weaker, hapless, helpless, at a loss, out of play. We rest, recover, regroup, take for granted unevenness of functioning, variability of being. There is a latent sense that we might make a wrong move, trip, fall through a trapdoor waiting to open, or already open and hungry, unfilled. We plunge time and time again, until the plunge becomes part of our heritage. We partly get used to it, but the fear does not vanish. Somewhat like fear of falling down. A child takes joy in the accomplishment of walking. Falling down doesn't stop him, it eggs him on. But in the background of being there remains a sense that one might fall. That one is some-how off balance, teetering, hanging on every step, until the other foot comes to the rescue.

Aner: If it remains, can we get used to being emotionally off balance?

Mike: We do and do not get used to it. Fear remains, partly because there is a boundless aspect to emotional life. Physically falling and picking one[self] up or getting picked up by another is fairly contained, specific, defined. A physical frame of reference is a relief, a blessing in face of inchoate fears. One of the reasons there can be so much terror in physical falls (especially the initial shock or jolt, being off balance, beginning to fall) is because of [the] unconscious emotional boundlessness, free fall, infinity of falling it triggers or taps into. There is a boundless aspect to emotional life that never finds a limit; a boundlessness that is part of the fear of breakdown, dread that it will never end, one will never get out of it, that breakdown is forever. People have their ways of avoiding breakdown areas. They move around, over, to the side of fragility, places they sense will give way and not support them. They exer-cise capacities, areas of strength that enable them to circumvent the worst. Adults spend a lot of time avoiding fear of weakness. They do not know what to do with fragility. They are not taught how to work with breakdown tendencies. They learn to toughen up, make do, get the hang of something that usually works well enough. There is a widespread tendency to try to hide deprived and deci-mated neighborhoods of self. Many people remain latently afraid of a major breakdown that will never happen. We are semi-phobic about ourselves, often for good reason.

If trauma hits as personality begins to form, a possible conse-quence is permanent fear of beginnings. Beginnings signify trauma. The process of beginnings is permeated by a dread of shattering, a sense that something awful is on the way. Incipient sense of self is permeated by premonition of getting smashed. Dread clings to awareness, a sense of shattering that cannot be mended. Fear of breakdown melds with fear of beginnings.

Aner: How does this process take place between the mother and her baby?

Mike: The mother tries to make up for and soften breakdowns the child cannot handle. The baby decimates itself and is decimated by states that are too much for it, states beyond processing or passing through. The mother is an auxiliary processor, or, at least, comforter, soother, helper. She tries to relieve the agony. She tries to locate and relieve the distress that precipitates agony. She tries to cushion the catastrophic impact of life. She tries to respond to the emotionally stricken baby or child before the mounting agony settles into a baseline of chronic torment. The baby who is helped to come through such troubled states gradually learns that emotional difficulty is something one *can* come through, even if not always without scars or deformations.

Winnicott (1971, p. 97) describes a situation in which the baby is in distress for x time before mother helps. The baby reforms, refinds its normal shape. Ditto for $x + y$ time. The distress, the deformation (everyday language speaks of a twist of mind or self or soul, getting bent out of shape) does not lead to lasting horrendous consequences. The baby returns to itself and goes on being. Winnicott, however, speaks of an $x + y + z$ time, a point of real damage. Ordinary consciousness returns and the baby goes on living, but something has altered. An alteration undergone through misery turns into permanent damage. Once entering the z dimension, one remains permanently afflicted. One mutates. One may be challenged by massive haemorrhage of personality, inner and outer dislocation and distortion. One is challenged by oneself, the kind of being one has become, may become. Not everyone is up to this challenge. Evasive measures are the rule. Some scour the psychic landscape for teachers. To learn what to do with oneself becomes a vocation, a calling. Quality of outcome depends, partly, on the luck of the link, the sort of teachers one stumbles on, the guides a society is able to offer for use. Occasionally one faces up to one's situation and begins the lifelong task of building resources to work with it.

Personality mutation or alteration can take one a long way from dread of beginnings. One gets buried in attempts to help oneself. Personality layers grow over and under each other and one becomes more convoluted, labyrinthine, opaque. Now and then one gets back to fear of beginnings, moments when the need to begin fingers nerves of existence. One has a chance to make contact with, taste intimations of a conjunction of fear of beginnings and fear of breakdown. Some stay at this meeting point, find a vocation there, a need to work with breakdown of beginnings, traumatized beginnings.

Aner: What does it take to begin?

Mike: To begin becomes a lifelong process, working towards beginning, learning to begin. One never begins fully and well enough, but makes inroads, learns a lot about saying hello to oneself, and possibly something about greeting others as well. One learns how to mutate better, to become a better mutant version of oneself, a mutant partner.

Problems with beginnings spread. Any sort of beginning can be afflicted: the start of relationships, a work of art, a book, a thought, a feeling or sensation. Abortion is a psychic state or inner force. If one is lucky, one learns a little about enabling bits of experience to undergo developmental arcs.

Unconscious support is a pressing issue. To feel and be supported in the background of one's being raises important questions. What kind of support, what quality? Grotstein writes of a background subject of primary identification (1981, 2000), a background presence. A warp pervading the background presence affects the feel of life, sense of life, one's psychic taste and smell, one's approach to life's horizons. If the horizontal frame is warped, what comes within or through it undergoes deformations. Consequences may be dynamic and structural, but also sensory. Many years ago (Eigen, 1993, Chapter Four) a patient told me about an anal scent that clung to the air, the taste of life, the marred look on faces, sounds of voices (sound smells, too), perhaps a faecal tint to everything. One day I spontaneously remarked, "It seems you can't stop living in your mother's asshole," and for moments the illusion/hallucination popped and he felt the difference. A competing frame of reference and life horizon was emerging. There really is such a thing as more or less fresh psychic air, taste, sound.

Aner: To sense and to unconsciously process goes hand in hand.

Mike: Yes. Problems with psychic sensing often involve problems in unconscious processing. We are supported by unconscious processes physically and psychically. If something is wrong with unconscious processes that support us, attempts to locate what bothers us often run amok. Physical medicine has an easier job. Disease processes in the body can be detected by various instruments. How life feels to us is more elusive. The instrument we have for communicating such important data is ourselves.

We say with poetic licence that something may be wrong with our psychic digestive system, that ability to take in and digest emotional states may be damaged. It is a way of speaking that has uses and limitations. It is a vision that brings out the sense that something is wrong with that which supports and keeps us in life. A concern in Bion's work is ability or failed ability to process catastrophic impacts. We nibble, choke, chew on bits of catastrophe, traumatized affect globs that freeze, paralyse, galvanize us, just like a fish nibbling on chunks of stuff that contain nutrient. Except it is unclear what nutrient catastrophic affects contain—perhaps simply ability to feel and the quality of that ability. Trauma destroys and nourishes. Traumatic impacts damage, kill, also wake us up, force us to other levels, other dimensions of living, for better and worse.

Aner: So much depends on our ability to process.

Mike: What I am saying simply (again) is that if unconscious affect processing is damaged, we live with chronic psychic indigestion or worse. One could say something similar using respiration, psychic breathing, and speak of asphyxiation, suffocating. In both cases we use images concerned with how we take in and let out. We express a sense of haemorrhage, being jammed, stuck, perhaps something explosive, a tendency to lash out. Common speech combines zeroing out and violence: striking out. In baseball, it is zero, nothing, you hit air, and you lose. In life, you hit others, not just a ball. Underneath is elemental self-assertion, e.g., striking out in a new direction, a new enterprise, a bit of individuality, a taste of freedom. There are moments when a baby strikes out at what bothers it, flailing blindly perhaps, unable to locate the source of disturbance. It lacks a frame of reference (mental map, psychomotor coordination) to do the job. Sometimes, it hits on a change of position, its own movements creating change of states. It experiences a range of success and failure at helping self and being helped by another, galaxies of possibilities. It lets a lot pass. You can't process everything, especially if you don't know what you're processing and lack equipment to do it. You work with the bucket or thimble you are.

Things tend to work by themselves, you in the mix. My guess is, as you grow you sense something not growing or growing wrong, ways you are stuck, like becoming aware of a body defect, a sense of self-deformation, not functioning right, not feeling right. Maybe you grow around it or with it if enough feels OK. You find areas of reality that work for you. You make up for the block, defect. Maybe the wound or damage stimulates certain kinds of development and use of talents.

Aner: Bion is very interested in what can and cannot be processed.

Mike: Bion writes of dream-work, more broadly, alpha function being damaged. Let me speak loosely. Alpha function is a term Bion coins to evoke awareness that there are unknown ways we process experience, ways we take experience in, attend to it, work with it, grow with it, allow it to become part of unconscious creativity. Dreams play a role in this processing. Dream-work nibbles at globs of experience, sometimes exquisitely beautiful experience, erotic, spiritual, affirming—providing tastes of life that open life. Dreams are part of and feed growth processes. Often they are concerned with disaster anxiety, catastrophic impacts, annihilation dreads, a sense of catastrophe too big too handle, too much for our physical frames, our psyche. Dreams try to break off bits of catastrophic dreads, work with them. We get inklings of this work through their images and narratives. One way to try to metabolize trauma is to split its affect, divide and conquer, project or externalize part of it via paranoid scenarios, particular dreads instead of nameless ones: someone is breaking in, going to kill you, violate you, cause some kind of damage that you can not control. Often the nameless, generic, global, formless aspect of background terror remains in the fact that the attacker is no one you know, anonymous terror assuming a particular form. You are helpless, veer towards paralysis, your scream does not come out, is not loud enough, cannot be heard. You wake up screaming. At least you yourself heard it, and, like a baby changing positions, you changed levels of consciousness. But the dream aborted. It could not handle the processes it tried to express.

Aner: Was it a real psychic abortion or did it just drop?

Mike: The something bad or awful happening was real on several scores. It points to a trauma history inscribed in the body, in the psyche; a trauma history dreams are concerned with. At the same time, dreams express something of the processes that go into make dreams, the fate of these processes, and news of their journey. There are, so to speak, messages of work in progress, and failed work in progress. A nightmare, at least, makes you feel the tension, the dread. The nightmare does not dismiss it. It does not wake up out of itself and say, "I am only a dream. I am not real". On the contrary, nightmare is gripping and, as it is going on, it is very real, hyper-real. It is saying: these feelings, states, issues are real. Unlike waking life, waking society that tries to diminish their impact and import, make light of them—only a dream, not real. Although for some, the feelings linger, one knows something is there.

Waking life makes fun of dream feelings, plays them down, and then starts a war maiming and killing hundreds of thousands of people. Waking life wipes the earth with blood. Which came first, the outside or inside nightmares? Once the cycle starts it almost doesn't matter. Except for one point: if we are right that truly working with the concerns of inside nightmares will diminish the need for outside ones, if we workers in psychic basements are at all correct in this it matters indeed, it matters a lot whether or not we can sustain dreams that need to be worked with, that tell about feelings that bother us, that disturb our peace, our imaginary wish for peace, trying to make room for what we fail to make room for.

Aner: So where are we stuck?

Mike: I am not sure. Are we stuck with an unsolvable situation: dream-work gets damaged by the dreams it tries to dream? Will affect processing always be maimed and disaster prone? I suspect so but, if partly so, it is good to let that in, make room for it. Failed dreams are like running starts. We keep at it through the ages, artists, scientists, mystics, politicians, psychoanalysts, ordinary dreamers, folk dreamers, part of a common attempt to build a cultural digestive system over the ages, to become better affect transmitters, processors, communicators, to become less damaging to ourselves, to become more inspiring.

Aner: Can we do it?

Mike: We are doing it now, unevenly, but we fear history is taking backward steps. Conservative forces are trying to put breaks on the amazing plasticity and fluidity we have discovered. Freud's postulation of libido expresses awareness of fluidity: a common energy that takes many forms. In religion it would be One God taking many forms. It is a fluidity that opens new channels in art, literature, science, a fuller transformational awareness spreading through many dimensions. There are conservative powers that fear the opening of the boxes, the melting of rigidities. Fundamentalists chop the One God taking many forms into oppositional camps. There are attempts to impose parochial will and strategy—whether as a super-power or shifting molecular groupings—on the open vision that is evolving. The fact that the same material can be solid, liquid, gaseous, that words and colours take on their own lives and lead to new places, that a touch or feel of a person can change our sense of skin, thought textures, the way movement tastes, that feelings turn into thoughts turn into sensations turn into art work, that scientists call the universe queer: will "they" seek to make our marriage to a queer universe illegal, will they succeed in outlawing the psyche? To destroy Buddhist statues in Afghanistan is one way to outlaw the psyche. If there is one thing we are fearfully good at, it is finding ways to damage ourselves. Our methods of doing this are exquisite and powerful indeed. Yet no method of destruction, no matter how thrilling or chilling, comes close to matching the beauty of a single Bach cello solo or an amazing building. We need to study the ways we destroy ourselves. We need university courses, perhaps departments, on self-destruction. This is something all the peoples of the world have to pool knowledge about, and more than knowledge, have to do something about.

Aner: Religion has acknowledged it and has a lot to say about purification from evil, sins, and destructiveness.

Mike: I agree with that. I think of the *tashlich* ritual of Rosh Hashana. Rosh Hashana, you know, is the Jewish New Year; thought of as the birthday of the world, a Day of Awe, part of a renewal sequence. The challah bread comes in the shape of a crown, acknowledging God's kingship. Emphasis is on beginnings, re-beginnings, resetting oneself, re-finding, re-centring, re-anchoring in the holy, in the ethical. I was taught it is like taking one's soul to the cleaners. We are told, too, that praying to God, repenting, is enough to atone for ritual sins, but for trespass against people, amends need to be made with the people themselves. It is, then, a time of repair, of reparation.

It is not surprising to find that water has a place. In the *tashlich* ceremony, we stand by a sea, a stream, some body of running water, and recite prayers of transformation. It is customary to empty our pockets into the stream, or shake the corner of our prayer shawl or *tsitsit*, or throw bread to the fish. Let the fish have our sins, let them disappear into the water. The Hebrew word *tashlich* literally means something like, "thou shalt cast", and refers to Michah 7:19: "Thou wilt cast all their sins into the depths of the sea."

To a mystical psychoanalyst this casting of sins into living waters has endless significance. In Micah, of course, it is God who does the casting, the throwing away. Of course, it is God who is THE living sea. We cast our sins into God. God cleanses us of sin. God teaches us to do as He does, to cast our sins into the waters of life. For our sins are the waters of life. And the waters of life are more than our sins.

The Days of Awe have a variety of casting out rituals, various modes of self-cleansing. The *tashlich* ritual is only one, but one of the most beloved. You can go to the water with a loved one, your family, the prayer community, or alone. It is a truly pleasurable, fun, and mysterious time to share with your kids, a time of appreciation of what life gives us, how we treat what life offers, our communion with nature, with God, with each other.

Aner: How do we treat the fish? I mean, can we ever stop injuring someone, something?

Mike: I'm not sure how we treat the fish. We feed them our sins. We joke about it. In reality, they and the ducks rush for our bread, everyone is happy. It is something we like to do, look forward to. But we do understand it is not possible to live without injury. It comes down to that, after all, that we injure each other, wilfully, or out of neglect, or simply because of our own life drive, the flow of life. This is central to our picture of sin: injuring others, whether out of malice or élan. It is utopian to think we can stop this. I've been horrified by people who claim to be cleansed of their sins (by Jesus, or prayer, or rituals, or good deeds) and do horrible things, often hypocritically, wearing moral masks. Injury does not stop. But our relationship to it can deepen, grow richer in appreciation for who we are and what we do, for what we can try to do. We can emotionally invest in our own depths, our own growth, our realization of how destructive we are, how destructive sheer aliveness can be.

Here is one meaning of the depths of the sea, of the fishes. I think this is one meaning of the Kabbalah story that God pulls back, contracts to make room for others. To make room for creation, for us. This is one of our great callings, a challenge: to make room for ourselves and each other, to create together a space we can inhabit, co-inhabit; co-habitation, to learn more about interweaving.

So we throw destruction into the sea polluting it with our sins. The fish represent the nibbling we do on our traumatized–traumatizing state, our attempt to take in, process, metabolize, transform, grow, do better with ourselves, with life. To live better here is not a pleasure imperative, but an ethical one. It is to live more care-fully, more fully caring. A great biblical imperative: to convert a heart of stone to a heart of flesh, to be of use, to help others as well as oneself. To what extent is this possible? We differ in our visions. Many of us do not believe the way to help others or ourselves is to kill people—unless self-defence absolutely requires it. But violence is not limited to economic and military life between nations. Abuse in families is rampant. Suicide is an international problem. Rosh Hashana says, repeatedly, we harm ourselves by harming others. We harm our beings, our souls, our ethical health, murder as ethical suicide. Sensitivity to others as well as self, an ethics of sensitivity, is essential for quality of being.

Aner: And the water—the deep unconscious? God?

Mike: So many life elements in *tashlich*: the living bread (an essential sacrament), living waters, living sins, living fish, living people. We are talking about participating in a lively processes; how to approach life in ways that are alive yet minimize injury. This is what learning is all about.

The substructure, that which supports us in life, is here symbolized by the depths, the water, the work of the inhabitants of the depths, the fishes, our attempts to digest our destructiveness, to make use of it, the nourishment inherent in destroying, the élan of power, the pleasure of injury. Sins are associated with pleasure *and* tragedy. They fuse. And in the waters of the unconscious, the waters of transformation, deep work goes on, mysteriously, out of sight.

Aner: Why not make the unconscious conscious, make it more under the dominance of the ego? Perhaps that can help.

Mike: To some extent, at least, we must rely on unconscious processing. Consciousness cannot do it all. Consciousness often gets in the way, makes the wrong decision, screws up. The idea of making the unconscious conscious can be misleading. Lying permeates conscious and unconscious processes. Making something conscious is no guarantor of truth. Indeed, consciousness may rip off its acquisitions, internal or external, or use its resources myopically, for strategic, selfish gain. The public sphere is polluted with political lies in the service of economic power. The so-called ego, too, can poison psychic resources in the service of self-aggrandizement. Neither consciousness nor unconsciousness has exclusive rights to truthing/lying. The self-confrontation we are called to is more radical than any formula suggests.

Since we use consciousness as an instrument, we have to keep it in good repair, clean it up, try to make it as serviceable as we can. But who is going to clean *us* up? Sometimes we sense something wrong with dream-work, sense unconscious damage, and consciousness works overtime trying to correct or make up for the deficiency or difficulty. This has its value, but often backfires. We become hyper-mistrustful of unconscious work and obsessively try to do it all ourselves, head-stuff, vigilant, hyper-consciousness. We can't let go and let unconscious work support us, because we know there is something wrong with us deep down, through and through. Yet we come to learn that unless something better happens in the sub-basement, attempts to heal ourselves go haywire. We damage ourselves by trying to help ourselves. Little by little, we catch on, sense the depth of the difficulty, lower ourselves like a kind of well bucket, begin to develop a more cooperative attitude with what is out of view. We can continue to rip ourselves off, but psychic colonialism takes its toll. Sooner or later, hopefully, we realize we need all the help we can get. Consciousness is in big trouble if the unconscious processes that support it run amok, and vice versa. Conscious and unconscious are threads of the same fabric. If something is wrong with the fabric, you will not be able to localize the blemish solely in consciousness or unconsciousness.

We appeal to dogma to escape entering more fully into mutually corrective and self-corrective work. Some of us feel a pressure to grope along with no solutions, yet develop a feel for materials that compose us and a sense of the realness of diverse claims. The depths can be transformed, somewhat, in a deeper interactive field. Dialectic of trust and distrust, faith and circumspection develops. It takes time and real work, but it makes a difference to discover that support comes from underneath and outside, from deep within and from the stranger, the neighbour. It is worth the time we put into creative work, into what we can contribute, our attempts—it is part of the pool of mutual growth, struggle, influence, care. We try to do what we can as part of the one wheel with many handles. Am I in danger of substituting one kind of formula for another, one impossibility for another? Am I merely uttering, muttering, stammering a perennial challenge that solutions break against like waves of the sea? I think of Bion's remark, "When two personalities meet an emotional storm is created". A common storm centre, the hub of the wheel we share.

The writing process

Aner: Tell me more about the writing process.

Mike: I learned as a young man I can't take too much writing at a time. I used to read about writers that go on and on. Too much tension for me. I remember an incident when I was younger.

I planned to write all weekend but became too anxious, then depressed. I couldn't take it and found myself on a plane heading for Paris. By the time I got back I knew I had to learn how to dole out the writing experience. I had to start from scratch and learn what works. Writing maybe two or three hours at a stretch was the most I could do before depression and disgust set in. People ask me how I write so much. A little at a time, intermittent doodling. The kind of depth communication I mediate requires a lot of intensity. How to dole out anything is a perennial challenge, no?

Aner: Do you find a difference in writing books like *Ecstasy* and *Rage, The Sensitive Self,* and *Emotional Storm* compared with The *Psychotic Core, Toxic Nourishment, Damaged Bonds,* and your more structured books?

Mike: All my books have written themselves. That doesn't mean I didn't work hard on them. I did work hard. But they grew their own ways, made their own demands. Poetry is in all of them. The sort of psychoanalysis I do includes, partly springs from, a poetic impulse. I regard most of the analytic writers I've immersed myself in as psychoanalytic poets of one sort of another. Bion's works are filled with compelling imagery, intuitive visions, rooted in clinical realities. Winnicott's appreciation of literature and the literary value of his work is well known. Form and structure vary in my books, but the poetic thread runs through them. Poetry as a mode of cognition, of course, but more than that, a mediator of emotive reality, a creator of expressive reality, part of the evolution of experiential capacity.

Aner: What were your motivations behind each of your books? How did you develop as a psychoanalytic writer?

Mike: *The Psychotic Core* was an act of communication growing out of realities I and others felt [to be] very important. It grew out of a course I taught at the National Psychological Association for Psychoanalysis. I tried to bring out the centrality of psychosis in much psychoanalytic work, inherent in Freud's structural concepts and clinical descriptions, at work in borderline, schizoid, and narcissistic individuals. Reference to the madness of life and our world is not vain. The chapters in *The Psychotic Core* were topics for classes. Psychosis was a marginal area in psychoanalytic training. It was not deemed as relevant, certainly not central for work with most patients. We have learned otherwise, and I try to convey this. Wittingly or not, psychotic dynamics permeate clinical work today.

After *The Psychotic Core* I had an urge to write more clinical portrayals and, if possible, in more detail. I picked non-psychotic individuals representative of what people are up against in society and themselves in today's world. I chose people I worked with earlier, partly to mask their identities, and only those I had verbatim session notes on. When I was younger, I went through periods of note taking as a kind of check on what I was doing. *Coming Through the Whirlwind* and *Reshaping the Self* are results of these studies. I felt driven to be as honest as possible which, at the time, meant as literal as possible, to get as close to sessions as I could, transmit them faithfully, say what happened, transcribe them, record them. It was a residue of taking Descartes' radical doubt literally, strip away everything to get at the real. It would take more living for me to realize that the Real was Everything.

In *Coming Through the Whirlwind* I wrote about a spiritually inclined woman whose erotic life upset the apple cart. I would look forward to session ends when we touched hands—shaking hands, it's called. Warmth, electricity, hunger, thrills. Hands shaking— trembling, quivering—was more like it. I died when we touched. I well understood the force that led to her affairs with ministers and wrecked her standing in religious communities.

When I met her, she felt guilty for wanting to explore herself. She felt spirituality should be enough. Psychology was murky, not godly. Little by little she let herself in and was able to use therapy to work with psychological difficulties that spirituality masked. The taboo against getting deeper into oneself, learning about oneself, is more severe than sex. It almost sounds as if the prohibition against self-exploration is akin to masturbation guilt and anxiety, except the former is more pervasive and difficult. We now have a President of the United States who is proud of his inability to explore himself, an example for the nation of good values.

To her and my surprise, my patient discovered her helping vocation as a lawyer for the disenfranchised. She also found that in her life, her path, spirituality and Eros were interwoven. Through our work, she better appreciated their connection.

The other person in *Whirlwind* was a therapist who used truth like an axe murderer. He used psychology as a defence against spirituality. He zeroed in on falsehoods in others, exposing them, rubbing their noses in his honesty. He lost girlfriends this way and was in danger of losing his wife and breaking up his family. With credit to him, he stuck with it and saw through his destructive use of psychological truth. He learned the difference between caring and brutal use of truth.

The understanding that leads to a kindly attitude toward others is more important than being right about what one sees, especially when the latter is a narrow band of vision.

In *Reshaping the Self*, I write about a woman schoolteacher who loves her work but has to fight to support her students and the work she loves in face of personality constricting bureaucracy. The job pinches and distorts her being and she must struggle to keep faith with creativeness in her students and herself.

A similar problem confronts my other patient in *Reshaping the Self*. A successful businessman hates the way he has to behave in order to remain successful. He loves being a businessman but does not like what his job is doing to him. In therapy he struggles with work, himself, societal and familial difficulties and hits on the "solution" of starting his own business in a town he likes better. Like others in these two books, he sought and found a more personalized way to make a living, a way to live a more personal life in general.

In both of these works I focus on distinction–union structures in self–other and mind–body relations in quite some detail. In *Reshaping*, too, there is an interesting aside on the contraction–expansion rhythm. I mention the Job story as a model of aspects of psychic work. Stripping everything away to a denuded point, then expanding. Of course, at the point of maximum contraction, Job sees God. He never stops seeing Him, but now sees Him with special apprehension, awestruck. A somewhat different experience from my alcoholic patient [see p. 65–68], but not altogether different.

Aner: What I found amazing about the businessman, is that this patient is very down to earth, he has not a single gram of spirituality in his character; I wonder how you two communicated.

Mike: I liked him. He was a little like a ten-year-old child I once worked with, who looked at therapy as a kind of detective mystery, something to figure out. My businessman was an extraverted, pretty decent guy. You wouldn't think he'd have much interest in the psyche. He produced conflict dreams, heroic dreams. In one series there was a war between a good and evil figure, a life and death struggle. In spite of his dread and the superior might of his antagonist (a sort of devil), he exerted all his strength, hope against hope, and came through, with support. He was meeting his fear of death, or trying to, and his fear of himself. I do think we are more afraid of ourselves than of death, although some people think the two fears are equivalent.

Aner: Did you feel that you stayed honest to the case, to the cases? Did you satisfy the impulse that led you to write these books? [*Coming Through the Whirlwind and Reshaping the Self*.]

Mike: I wasn't satisfied. I did stay honest to the case, the cases, and the cause: that is, I wrote these cases close to the letter of the happening, the way they occurred in sessions. As close as I could. There's a lot there. The writing worked. But I learned that the feel of reality, what really happens, remains elusive, comes through between, beyond, beneath the words. You can't literalize the psyche. You can't nail the psyche to words—she said he said—in a concrete way. "Honesty" is not enough. Psyche bursts through, catches you, and realizes itself through holes in your net. These books, like all others, overflow with psyche that letters can't contain. You can use words like bait. The fish are another matter. Water is filled with them. The fish eat the words that catch them, the words eat the fish. The fish disappear, words do too. The most important things are always left out.

Years later I read in Bion that no literal documents can convey the affect of the session. The analyst almost has to be a poet, an artist, for the feeling of the session to find expression on a page. How can what you write do justice to the emotional truth of a session? You have to write from the affect, let it speak. It's not a matter of literal or figurative writing. All my writings are ways of trying to get through to the reader, subject to subject, self to self, mind to mind, heart to heart. The reader is crucial. Perhaps you know what I mean, since you are drawn to my work. My words are snakes or birds or fish mediating psychic reality. Hopefully, psychic reality survives my attempts and you and I survive psychic reality. More than survive, [discover] a richness worth working for.

Aner: *Rage, Ecstasy, The Sensitive Self,* and *Emotional Storm* were written later in your career. Is it because these poetic books needed more courage and maturity to publish them?

Mike: It looks that way. Maybe there's an element of that, but that's not the way I experienced it. My experience was that each time I wrote something it was the thing that came up to write. Sometimes you get an idea from a session, something someone said, something you read, something you heard. *Ecstasy* grew out of something I've sensed since I was a child, something I heard in myself. The feeling of a most valued experience, as when I first saw stars in the night sky, or kissed a girl who made me tingle, or first heard a clarinet play Yiddish music. The list goes on, but is not huge. It is a feeling that makes life worthwhile.

I was happy when the book finally came knocking, pressing, saying, "It's my turn now. I'm next". I had been waiting a long time to write on ecstasy, front and centre, my personal centre. A relief—long awaited. The surprise was the space in the book devoted to destruction. The more I got into it, the more I had to write about the melding of ecstasy and destruction. I thought I was going to write an affirmation—ecstasy as the heart of experience, a pivot. Little did I know that the Muse or Angel or Demon of writing was setting me up to give voice to ecstatic destruction, menace, horror. A voice of trauma, devastation—the evil we gladly inflict on one another and ourselves.

There's a positive core to the psyche, and a positive core to my book, *Ecstasy*. But it is not a simple business. All my work conveys need for struggle, hardship, and confrontation of oneself. At the same time, there is a deep shining, opening.

Aner: *Rage* seems like ecstasy's destructive twin.

Mike: *Rage* carries the melding of ecstasy and destruction forward. Rage is addictive. Few experiences are more total. Rage is a good example of an orgasmic current in destructiveness. There is something orgasmic about all-out rage. Often it builds, climaxes, and becomes blinding—blinding rage, a blinding storm.

A sense of right often permeates rage, a sense of being right about being wronged. Rage partly fuses with and obliterates pain, a kind of pain orgasm. It is a fury at being wounded and a wounding fury. Destructiveness often fuses with imaginary purity, attempts to clean away bad stuff, a cleansing through violence, and a destructive sense of justice.

In *Rage*, I analyse God's personality, write about the human scream, connect some of the dots having to do with rage and psychic terrorism. The link between rage and cleansing persists unabated. A few days ago I read about two teenage boys beating another boy with a steel bar and an ice pick, leaving him in critical condition. They tried to beat the hell out of him, cleanse him, cleanse their own lives from his polluting presence because he had blue hair and wore an inverted cross, mark of Satan. I believe unconscious and semi-conscious hallucinating and delusional thinking is part of blinding rages. A gruesome fact is that today what once might have been momentary rage gets strung out over time, threaded through long-term calculation and technological know-how.

Our mad psyche is permeated by idealizing tendencies, a sense of purity, a sense of beauty. So much that ennobles us, that lifts life and fills it with colour and makes it worthwhile, adds to human madness and misery. We are quite mad. Even our sanity is dangerous. The link between sanity, sanitize, sanitation, cleaning up your act, is a wish to somehow get out of our messy plight. In *Emotional Storm*, I try to show that we need to get used to our upheaval, learn to work within the storm, become better storm sharers, storm processors. Getting out of it, rising above it does not seem to do the trick. We need to enlarge processes of receptivity, become better storm partners.

We are heading for pretty eerie storms, since reality is turning into a form of entertainment. I suppose it always has been fodder for profit and power. But with current techno-ability, our perennial plight of deformed or stunted emotional and mental development can cause more damage, even approximate that age-old orgasmic fantasy of wiping human consciousness clean out of existence, the abortion or clean-up that most titillates righteous rage. The current political regime in my country has almost succeeded in turning war into a form of power entertainment, but I suspect the pain of real bodies will eventually break through. War as a beatific feed blotting out for a time real misery. "Mission Accomplished!"

There is a loving imperative that I don't want to hurt my children more than I have to, and that I want to diminish this "have to". "Have to" thinking should be subject to systematic mistrust, an occasion for analysis. The war worth fighting is the ongoing struggle with one's psychotic self, with destructive displays of affect and thought, with the sense that I have a right to inflict my deformations on others. If I'm neurologically destined to kill my children or yours, then I am required to fight my neurology, to battle my physiology, to alter my internal environment by opposing it, by engaging it. I am required to do this and you are, too. What dictates this imperative? Simply, a sensitive sense of each other and ourselves. To employ destruction for good, an age-old calling, wish, necessity. And this good? That's what we fight about.

Light

Aner: Light and a radiant "I-kernel" seem to be key elements in understanding how you work with people.

Mike: This has been so since my first article, "Abstinence and the schizoid ego", published in 1973 in *The International Journal of Psycho-Analysis*, [and] collected by Adam Phillips as a chapter in *The Electrified Tightrope*. I portrayed an alcoholic man who weaned himself from the bottle by going through severe withdrawal from himself and the world, an extreme contraction, which spontaneously issued into an expansion, a radiant sense of life. This was a plain, uneducated man who came to me through a clinic. Alcoholics Anonymous was important, but did not do the trick. He would cycle between getting off drink (everyone rooting for him), then falling into the gutter (everyone sad). Therapy somehow gave him permission to go through what he needed, touch bottom and beyond (discover bottomlessness), and re-establish himself. This happened without specific religious content. Freud's letters to Fliess has similar imagery when he describes aspects of his creative processes, blocks, impasse, loss of orientation, darkness, blindness, breakthrough of light. From time to time, Freud used religious and mystical imagery to describe creative experience. Perhaps we could say religious imagery is one way we give form to creativeness.

Aner: So what made for your patient's change? How did this happen?

Mike: I'm not sure. It was a surprise to both of us. I doubt it could have happened without his link to Alcoholics Anonymous but it couldn't have happened without therapy either. People tend to get you away from yourself. As if there's widespread fear of making contact with what's there. Even in AA, he couldn't quite open up without getting attacked, misunderstood, pushed. We are phobic about ourselves. Maybe it was a combination of the community he got from AA and the deeper understanding and permission he got from therapy.

By that time I knew something about the Light. I knew it was there. I knew it could appear anywhere, anytime, to anyone. Whether or not it would was another question. It's not something I push on people, but if it happens I'm receptive. I certainly am not going to sponsor it as a cure for alcoholism. I meet each moment as it comes. This attitude sometimes angers people. It angers my wife when she tries to get me to say I made a decision in marrying her, in fathering children. It doesn't feel that way to me. It feels like it just happened. It grew. I'm glad it happened. I helped it along. But it was as much a surprise to me as the darkness and light journey my patient went through. I did not expect him to get cured by seeing me. I did hope I could help him live better somehow, maybe help him be a better alcoholic. The process, once started, had its own momentum. He was able to marry someone in the AA programme after our experience. It took me longer and I wish I [had] married sooner. But a lot of work had to be done. I was not ready. I had not yet reached the point of realizing I would never be ready and you have to begin, dive in, ready or not.

I was deeply moved by my patient's descent, withdrawal, contraction. As if he had to detoxify himself, not from drugs or alcohol but from himself, from the world, from people, from his own personality, his own impingement on himself. I think I provided him space to withdraw from himself, to leave himself in peace a little, to stop nagging himself. To stop nagging himself into health, to stop being persecuted by having to get better. Thinking you have to be healthy is one of the great diseases of our time.

The patient and I were astonished by a radiant I-kernel at the point of maximum contraction and after a pause, a beatific expansion, a radiant world, akin to the in–out of breathing, with its caesuras, expansion, and contraction. It was a pulsing shared by I-feeling. At the time, I linked my patient's experience with Guntrip's writings on the "schizoid ego", a passive, needy, withdrawn aspect of self or tendency seeking the imaginary quietude of the womb. My patient's withdrawal, however, culminated in transcendent radiance, active in its vibratory, pulsing, thrilling way, ultimately encompassing self and world.

I went on to explore workings of this transcendent ego when things went wrong, a kind of mocking "heh-heh" devil, occultly megalomanic, sardonic spirit or attitude, above the body ego, persecuting the latter. Persecutory, controlling, manipulative hate-filled transcendence lording it over a passive/impulsive/explosive body self. In *The Psychotic Core*, I took this to be a presiding structure of our time. This was in the 1980s and still is so, although things have taken a somewhat different turn. Psychopathic manipulation of psychotic anxieties have increased in importance and effectiveness—an Age of Psychopathy rather than merely madness.

Aner: The "heh-heh" devil? The part that ridicules?

Mike: Yes. Kleinians speak of the ego's contempt for psychic processes, for others, for life. Contempt for the good object, in their terms. I have somewhat amplified this clinical observation. At the same time, another thread of my work elaborates on positive effects of beatific or ideal experiencing. Many of my essays bringing out positive, healing aspects of "idealization" are collected in *The Electrified Tightrope*, essays on the face, faith, positive aspects of negative tendencies. It has become fashionable to see the good as a screen for desire or as a repressive force (which it can be). But—and I don't mean to abuse words—desire is desirable because of a certain goodness in it. The goodness of goodness is a thread that runs through my work, taking different turns, e.g., the last chapter of *Toxic Nourishment*, "Desire and nourishment".

Aner: How did this process occur with the alcoholic man?

Mike: With the alcoholic man I was speaking about, the process was terrifying. Every moment of every session tested our faith in a good or decent outcome. Any moment, things can go wrong, devastating, lethal. Lethal processes always were at work. Somehow we withstood them. Somewhat like people in his life, I provided a cheering section, happy when he was OK, sad when he went down. A difference was [that] I wasn't pushing him to get out of what he got into but to experience it and, if possible, share the experience with me. Tell me about it, of course. But there were other forms of contact and transmission. A look, tone, gesture—the affect in the room said everything. Self to self impact is the core clinical work.

I guess what happened is an example of what I called the distinction–union structure (in *The Psychotic Core*, *The Electrified Tightrope*, *Coming Through the Whirlwind*, *Reshaping the Self*). I was quiet a lot and, often without comment, would undergo the emotion in the room: the pain, hope, despair, abysmal misery, pleasures, gestures of joy. I suppose what I did was make room in me for him, to the extent I was able. As I said before, when something bad happened, I felt bad, when something good happened, I felt good. But I didn't lay these states on him. They were mine as well as his, once given. I lent a background cushion that registered emotional impacts. At the same time I knew his ups and downs were part of a mostly, but not entirely, unconscious pattern, perhaps going back very early in life. He went through cheering and disappointed parents, exaggerated plenitude and loss, storm and depletion. He was a child who hit on raising and deflating hopes, filling out emotional sails, windless. We talked about all sorts of things. His self-hate, bad self feelings, his need to excite and disappoint. He scared himself with his self-destructiveness, the greatest excitement of all. His destructiveness didn't get the same excited rise out of me that he was used to. People in his life got frightened for him. When he scared himself he felt their fear more than his own. I think now, because of my distance aspect, my difference, distinction, he could feel his own fear of himself more. He gorged on destructiveness, then became anorexic towards it. He recoiled, withdrew from himself, from his destructiveness, his toxic threat to his own life. The *Upanishads* speaks of the self no bigger than a thumb tip. My feeling is we tasted that self at the vanishing point, an indestructible I-kernel ultimately made of radiance that contracts and spreads.

Aner: How close are you to the most fundamental psychoanalytic work assumption: "Look in the patient's past". If you see a patient that suffers from deadness feelings would you not think of his past in terms of the patient's early relations with his mother?

Mike: That would be part of it, his trauma history, the life that drove him mad, that deadened him. But it is not simply in the past that he will get better. An important part of getting better will have to do with the emotional life we have together now, a growing sensitivity to impact and response. How we process our impacts on each other. I'm not sure any profession or societal group has focused so expectantly and minutely on moment to moment impact and response, their meanings, juxtapositions, changes, transforms. It is a kind of new discipline to see what we do to and with each other, sitting together, experiencing, speaking, sensing. The more to come, an element of time, protects against finality: no word the last. The past speaks, too, must speak. Even frozen time, heartless time, has ways of speaking. Hearts of past *and* future beat with us. We count on the next moment.

Aner: It seems that you don't necessarily have the need to understand every symptom in terms of childhood history?

Mike: History is always present, always working. Are there ahistorical processes? The word "every" makes me uncomfortable. Also, so-called "understanding" can be suffocating. People don't like to get put in boxes. Of course, feeling understood is important in its own right and makes one feel cared for. To understand enlivens, quickens, questions, reconciles, opens. But the understanding game is a dangerous business. Too often it is part of one-upmanship, analytic self-protectiveness, an attempt to control psychic life, cut it off prematurely.

People differ in their need for understanding. Some feel stuffed or threatened, some cared for, nourished, some feel deprived without it. Understanding can be part of the influence game, a power struggle, or a genuine light, a freeing moment.

There are all kinds of relationships to understanding, all kinds of qualities and uses of it, reactions to it.

Aner: What about yourself? Do you have a need to know?

Mike: Not as much as I should (laughs). I drift with an awful lot of uncertainty. I don't like to box people in. But it is not possible to be category free. Understanding is nourishing. Truth is nourishing. Love of truth, love of understanding: a great nourishing, driving force, but great tyrants too. How much destruction is unleashed by the way we understand things, by truths we live and die for. To sit together and speak about what we do to each other with our truths, the emotional impacts truth has on us: this is one of the contributions therapy can make to culture. The idea that we can do this and keep on doing this without coming to a conclusion, the notion of interminable analysis or therapy, is itself therapeutic, a guard against forcing ourselves and others into tyrannical finality. Another double capacity and need: to focus on what is unbudgeable while working provisionally along lines that yield access.

Aner: "In my life, Light just happened. I did nothing to find it. I did not even know it existed beforehand. I'm not sure it made me a better person. It didn't come because I was terrific. I'm glad it became a real presence for me. I don't know what I'd have done without it. How poor and empty things might have been without it" (*Ecstasy*, p. 98).

I know it must be very personal but I still hope you can elaborate on the idea of the light. I wonder if you want to add more to that.

Mike: It is personal. When I write my books I write what there is in me to say from my being. I give it expression which I doubt I can surpass now. It's personal for me because it happened to me but it's not limited to me, It is something that many people have experienced. It's personal in a sense that is transpersonal, across persons. It would not surprise me to learn that more people have these experiences than don't. Maybe people don't know what to make of them. I surely didn't know. I have lived with it a very long time, developed relationships with it. It's something that seems to have been recorded since antiquity. People had experiences like this in one form or another from the earliest times. It's an invitation, a shock that draws one into mystery, into the challenge of what a person can experience, including a sense that life is shockingly wonderful, whatever else it also is.

Aner: When I read this paragraph I felt that I was closely attached to you. I don't know if my light is your light. Maybe it's different. But there is something to share.

Mike: What a beautiful thing to say. Thank you. In the beginning of *Ecstasy* I write about a famous night when Pascal had a fire experience. A spiritual fire, a God fire awed him and he said "O my God You are real, God of Abraham, Isaac, Jacob—a burning reality". He was thrown into a new dimension. He had a transforming affect. For the Buddhist there's another framework, for the Hindu or Moslem another. There's no one way to approach such experience. But I think one thing common to all approaches is a sense of appreciation. When you say you feel we share light in same and different ways, we share appreciation of ourselves and each other. A light lifts us together. Now I wonder if a reason you are attracted to my work is because of light you breathe there.

Aner: It's very extraordinary to think that such paragraphs were written by a psychoanalyst and an American one, too. God, light,

Satan are mentioned in psychoanalytic journals only to describe pathology.

Mike: As a writer I am trying to give expression to what is trying to get expressed. Lots of experiences knock at the door, compete for expression, and I have to turn some down, not because I think they are unimportant but because it is too much. Not enough time or energy or ability. Sometimes I feel here's one that must be helped towards expression, but I draw back out of fear, a lack of strength and capacity. Sometimes I become afraid because I fear I've gone too far. Eigen, this time you've done it, it's too much. If only I were that lucky more of the time. The reality is, one usually does not go far enough and one pulls back prematurely. Where the Light is concerned, I don't know how one *can* go too far.

CHAPTER TWO

Life

A *ner*:   One of the most interesting things in your writings is
how the erotic experience and the intellectual experience
collide.

Mike: When I was younger, sexual experience was a spiritual
experience, and spiritual experience was very passionate. When I
was a sophomore in college, I met Socrates, the first person who
used the word Truth that I believed. Within a few months of opening to the thrill of Truth through Socrates, I had sexual intercourse
for the first time. I still meditate on the link between meeting
Socrates and making love, love of Truth and Eros, capacities that
keep interweaving.

There were differences between them but there were also big
areas of overlap. There were periods in my life when there was
conflict between them. I went through Augustinian struggles, flesh
against spirit, civil war. Why wasn't I more spiritual? What's all this
attachment to the realm of the flesh, the sensuous? The truth was I
never had a sexual relationship I didn't love. Sex brought me closer
to God, opened my heart. I saw God when I had sex. It just
happened.

Aner: What did God look like?

Eigen: (laughs). No image. No form. Sometimes light. Sometimes feeling. Sometimes a sensation, a God-sensation. There's such a thing, you know.

Aner: How did you start your career?

Mike: I had no interest in a career, none at all. My interest was the human soul. My first exposure to formal psychology was a flop. I hated dissecting frogs and explaining things in terms of reflexes. Two paragraphs in my psychology textbook grabbed me, one on gestalt psychology, the other on psychoanalysis. I liked thinking of wholes as the spontaneous self-distribution of parts and I valued intuition of unconscious processes. I had a hard time deciding whether to major in English or philosophy and ended up taking as many philosophy as literature courses. I guess I chose English because I felt, at the time, it came closest to the soul.

Aner: What books inspired you at that period?

Mike: When I was a senior, I started reading Suzuki and got into Zen Buddhism and Jung. When I was a junior, a friend told me a dream interpretation his Jungian analyst made and I lit up, bells rang, thrills. A lifelong love of dream interpretation began as an electric thrill. About eight months after I graduated college, I went into analysis with the man whose dream interpretation lit me up. I read Jack Kerouac and felt inspired to go on the road. I was taken by Eugene O'Neill's life in Provincetown on Cape Cod, Massachusetts and went there on my motorcycle. I was taken by D. H. Lawrence's writings on Mexico and went there for half a year, where I played in a band and wrote. I ended up in North Beach in San Francisco.

Aner: Were you travelling alone?

Mike: I did a lot of travelling alone, although sometimes with others. My father was very worried because he didn't know what was happening to me and because he was a very anxious person. I can understand his worries now that I have children. I hated his worries then. I paid him back for what I felt was over-anxiety. I kept him in suspense and lived my own life.

I became "counterphobic" and did many dangerous things and am lucky I survived those years. I almost did things to prove I wasn't afraid of anything. He was afraid, not me. I did crazy things with my motorcycle, walked on the outside of bridges, tempted fate a hundred ways. But the risks weren't only physical. I took Descartes's doubt seriously and tried to strip away everything. Radical doubt. I didn't understand the context of doubt as a method. I applied it to everything in my life. The adult world did not hold up very well. So much seemed phoney. One thing that did hold up was beauty. I could not reduce my experience of Beauty. I practised trying to wipe beauty out. Once I stared at a tree, determined to defeat its beauty, strip it of beauty. After some success, the feeling of overwhelming beauty surged through me. This was real. My thinking could not destroy my feeling of how beautiful things were.

Aner: When you did all these dangerous things, weren't you really frightened deep inside?

Mike: Oh, yes. But I pushed it aside. It took many years to begin appreciating the value of fear. The feeling that something terrible might happen is part of the thrill. A sense of putting oneself in danger and coming through. My writings on trauma involve coming through destruction over and over again. There was a sense of danger, relief, danger, relief. An attempt to live something through that has a hold on your soul.

Aner: Tell me about your conversations with your father at that time.

Mike: We didn't have many conversations for a number of years. I lost contact with him.

Aner: What kind of person was your father?

Mike: He was kind of a pathologically loving father, overprotective. On the other hand, he was not there because he was working hard. I didn't get to do things with fathers American kids often do. He was into work, study, raw affection, not sports. He didn't have the patience to sit through a movie. I never felt understood by him. Something different in us didn't click. His was a kind of love without respectful boundaries. When he was home, he expected me to do favours for him, pick up bottles at the bar or liquor store. Eventually I defended myself against endless requests, but learned a lot about people from the corner bar. I didn't realize that his outbursts were partly tied to liquor. My mother would hide his bottles and there were running battles about this. I didn't put together the liquor and rages that frightened me. I just thought that was the way he was and hated him. Overprotective and rageful, what a hurtful combination. It squelched, compressed, deformed me. I think part of my energy involves a wish to be free, to push past confines, burst through a sense of being held back. Break through the suffocation of fear, his and mine, my mother's goodness, my self-strangulation.

Aner: Was your father violent?

Mike: There was some violence, some hitting. That ended when I got to be a teen. I remember an incident when he raised his hand and threatened to hit me and I felt a surge of strength and put my hand up and that was the end of these kinds of threats. He never lifted a hand to me again.

Aner: What made him angry?

Mike: One of the things that made him angry was my making noise in the morning. Waking him got him upset. Noises, disturbance, things that interrupted his routine, his peace. My father was a very loving person, very emotional, physical; there is a lot of toxic love, a lot of warmth, but not a hell of a lot of understanding, not what Winnicott called percipience. He didn't really know who I was, didn't know me. I was a picture in his mind, an appendage of his ego. I used these words "appendage of his ego" when I was very young, before I knew about psychology. These words came to me when I was a little child.

Aner: Was your father spiritual?

Mike: When I was a kid, I was the one who went to *shul* (synagogue). I tried getting him to go with me but he preferred staying in bed on Saturday mornings. He told me, "God means good." God means doing good, helping others. As a kid, I didn't see him going to *shul* but I did see him helping others. He helped many people over rough spots in life. It was perhaps a kind of materially orientated help but it was more than that, too.

Yet our house was not devoid of religion, in negative and positive ways. He told stories about rabbis in the old country. One, in particular, stayed with me, about his mother taking her sick babies in the wintry cold to the rabbi (a particularly holy man) for healing. The trip made them worse. He and his sister were the only two of eight children who survived. For many years he told me what charlatans the rabbis were, although he must have known it wasn't the rabbi's blessings that killed them.

Aner: Was he religious? Did he have a religious lifestyle?

Mike: Well, not that I could see, not in the usual sense, not until he was much older. When he was older, he'd chant the Haftorah (i.e., the reading of the prophets) at Sabbath and holiday services. He enjoyed chanting later in life and read Hebrew easily. In my childhood, if we had a Seder it was because I said, "Let's have a Seder." He'd speed read the Haggada and in three minutes the Seder was over. Yet when rabbis came for donations, he'd drop everything, take out his checque book, and sit with them. There was one who came once a year who had a very special presence, a special holy glow, radiance; Rabbi Kelner, who had a face unlike any other. A kindly, intelligent, human face that made you quiver, thaw, which lifted you. It put me in touch with a dimension other than the struggle for existence, something at the centre of life incredibly beautiful, precious, holy, a sacred sense at the heart of life. It is only now I can begin to verbalize something of that feeling his face conveyed—more than devotion, awe, a genuine love of holiness, of God. Much later, in my forties, I read biblical passages about the Hebrews called to be a nation of priests, and something fell into place. "God said, 'You are holy because I am holy'." The sacred core of human life. I think I always felt it. I think many people do.

Aner: You really loved your father.

Mike: Yes, very much, yes. Love and hate.

Aner: Did you ever have a chance to talk with him?

Mike: Many times. He apologized and regretted very deeply the way he was when I was a child. He was horrified that he once held the belief that children's feelings didn't matter, that only adulthood mattered. It is no accident I am writing a book called *Feeling Matters*.

He was apologetic for the kind of person he was but couldn't help being. He understood it was a result of steeling himself to push past harsh beginnings. It's as if I remained sensitive to the damage in childhood he pushed past. You don't outgrow this kind of sensitivity. The latter has to undergo its own evolution. When I became a father I was acutely aware of [the] damage personality inflicts, the impact of one self on another. You can't escape it, but try your best to not make it worse than it has to be. Struggle with oneself pays off. My kids are much less damaging intersubjectively than my father or I. My father's ethics was, in a way, more externally orientated, behavioural. Good heart, good deeds, yes. But not attuned to possibilities of intersubjective affective transmissions, damage affective attitudes transmit from insides to insides, emotional damage.

Aner: Do you think that he felt sorry for his outbursts? Was there a sorrow moment?

Mike: I'm not sure if he felt that when I was young. Maybe as part of the cycle of emotionality exacerbated by drink, but not in a way that led to personality change. Many years later he felt more genuinely sorry. Much later, he was able to see himself from another perspective.

Aner: Your grandfather had a candy store. It's a dream come true for every kid.

Mike: I rarely got the sweets I wanted. Almost always he gave me Indian nuts, hard little nuts that were hard to open. I wondered if he gave them to me because no one wanted to buy them or because he really thought they were a treat or maybe better for you. Did he really think a little boy would like them? Maybe he wanted to toughen me or show how tough life is. Give me practice [in] meeting challenges, work hard at getting nourishment. He opened them effortlessly. Is that a paradigm of sorts, things that seemed easy for others felt difficult for me?

One day I saw a silver police whistle and he gave it to me. Finally, he gave me something I desired. Life is thrilling. I blew it like crazy, half expecting all the traffic on the street to stop. Blowing a silver whistle, stopping the world. But life went on as usual except I had a sliver of silver joy, a sense of getting lucky in a sea of frustration.

My grandfather made bathtub gin during Prohibition and sold it to the cops. He also sold illegal lottery tickets. These were tough times with no safety nets. Survival was up to you. Family love, yes, but harsh beginnings. My father told me stories about getting food from garbage in Vienna. He would run back and forth, ferrying food between lines of soldiers (First World War). A very difficult beginning.

Hard nuts, tiny eatable insides in tough and difficult shells, not always worth the trouble of opening. Trauma tough, crazy sensitive insides pushing into life, looking into corners with fear. No, it wasn't miserliness so much as insensitivity unconsciously transmitting what happens to a person. Life as hard and nutty. An awful communication. A casual enactment, demonstrating the precision of unconscious transmission in everyday life. Now I see hardening and cracking magnified in the world at large.

Aner: What about your father's mother?

Mike: I never met her. She died in the old country. They left her behind. She was supposed to come once the men were settled but she got sick and died during that time. My father had mixed feelings about her. He idealized her as a saint. From the nothing she had she would give to poorer people. Anger and bitterness ran through him, never directly about her. His sister came after their mother died, and I knew her very well. She had a strong bitter streak. Kind but bitter, a deep sense of deprivation. She resented my father for not taking care of her, as if he could make up for her difficult beginnings. Maternal neglect and paternal absence got displaced on to him. She wanted him to give more and always felt she didn't get enough. In fact, he helped her come to New York and find places to stay and sent money to her and her husband long after they married. I'd visit them in the Bronx when I was a kid. It was a thrill to take a bus from Passaic to New York and go to a Horn and Hardart automat, where food lit up in little transparent boxes and you put nickels in slots and lifted glass panels.

Her husband loved caring for beautiful tropical fish. They also had an old victrola that played music when you turned the handle. It was like a retreat, getting away from Passaic, away from my family, another view and taste of life. She took these opportunities to say bad things about my father. Why didn't he help more? Why did he leave her and her mother to a life of great hardship? Why didn't they (father and brother) bring them to America sooner?

Aner: Why did the family split?

Mike: Often males established the beachhead, got a place, got a job, got things ready. Then the women arrive.

Aner: Did they suffer from anti-Semitism?

Mike: Yes. It was part of life and its effects never went away. When I named my second son Jacob, my father tried to talk me out of it. He insisted, even after sixty years in the USA, that a name like Jacob would brand him for life. Who would have thought that by the time Jacob was a teen, his would be the most popular name in the country. "Nothing good can come of it", my father probably would think.

My father had lots of different jobs. He was filled with immigrant energy, the push of fear, the joy of promise. A candy store could not contain him. I have a photo of him as a teenager selling clothes. He wanted to take my girlfriends shopping, sure he knew clothes, but they found ways of getting out of it, knowing their tastes differed.

He didn't like American schools. He thought they weren't serious. Why so much sports and making little boxes with toys in them? You come to school to play? So he ended up leaving high school, studying on his own, and passing a state exam. He bought a used accounting book and got local businesses to hire him to keep their books. He put himself through law school that way. He loved law but hated the way people misused it. He wanted to be a chess player but knew he couldn't make a living "pushing the pieces". All through my childhood there were men in my house playing chess. He was proud of his national ranking. When I taught at Reuben Fine's institute, I asked Reuben, a renowned chess master as well as psychoanalyst, to play a correspondence game with my father. They played many games and I felt happy to provide my father with such a thrill.

Aner: Who were your father's friends in America? What was his social milieu?

Mike: They were immigrants like him. Many were Jewish, but not all. When he came here he spoke mainly Yiddish, German, and Russian. He could have learned English in Vienna but he refused because he was afraid he would have a foreign accent. He didn't want to sound like a greenhorn, an immigrant. He learned English when he came here and didn't have an accent.

In his old age he fell in love with Italy and learned Italian. He liked to tell about the time he spoke Italian to an Italian judge, and the judge asked what part of Italy he came from. The people in Passaic were Italian, Jewish, Polish, Irish, Eastern European. I knew rich people existed but I didn't know any. People struggled to make a living.

Most people I knew helped each other or left each other alone, but I ran into gratuitous cruelty which, in retrospect, probably was anti-Semitic. My father became disillusioned with the practice of law. He put a good deal into his work and expected similar integrity in others. He never got used to people cutting corners, taking advantage, one way or another screwing you. I often heard him say he liked to study law, not practise it, and would have liked to teach it. In his late years, after he retired, he took pleasure writing a column in a law publication.

Aner: Tell me about your mother.

Mike: She was born on the Lower East Side of New York City in 1912. Her parents came from Poland. Her mother spoke Yiddish and never learned English. Her father, on the other hand, learned English. He saw himself as a businessman. How much of a businessman he was God only knows. He had a pushcart at some point and did other things that I don't know about. I'm not sure when he left New York City for Garfield, New Jersey, which is where I lived during my first year or two. He was always selling this, buying that, making deals of one or another sort.

Aner: A Jew.

Mike: Yes, a Jew, but a poor Jew. He never had anything in a material sense but provided for his family. They had a roof over their heads, food, and the first two of his four children (my mother was first) went to college. They moved from a rooming house, to a two-family house, and by the time I was three or four, they had a house of their own.

When I was younger I had some dreams of being outside of places, reflecting outsider feelings. I remember in real life standing outside a big brick building, a hospital, my grandfather inside dying of heart failure, which probably could be treated today. I heard he drowned of water in his lungs. He was in his forties but looked like an old man. A story I heard many times was that he asked his nurses and others who visited, "I'm a rich man. You want to see my treasure?" They would give him funny looks. "No, no, come and see," he would say and take out my picture from under his pillow. I was the first of the grandchildren, the only one he would know, the first to be born in the new country. There was a background unconscious loading—grandparents I scarcely knew, relatives known and unknown, old country and new, a background texture I took for granted and later came to appreciate. Bits of memory, good and bad, would come unexpectedly through the years. A rich sensuous texture with a feeling running through not unlike the sense I had of the holy man I spoke about, Rabbi Kelner. My grandfather and grandmother (on my mother's side) had it in their own ways. It ran through the family.

Aner: What exactly was this feeling?

Mike: . A sense of preciousness, of the children being precious, something in life being precious, even if hard and harsh, something precious in the living soul. Later in life it came back to me that my grandfather felt my life was precious. So I could feel an unconscious sentiment, an unconscious backing, even though my particular interests and personality were off the radar screen of wheeler-dealers. There was a building up in my being of something valuable I was not aware of. You may ask: how can you speak of unconscious feeling—how do you know it if it's unconscious? That's an aporia we live with. You can rationalize and say there are different levels of conscious–unconscious being. But that does not touch what I am touched by. A lot happened that made me feel bad about myself, but another system was building too, the sense that there is something precious inside. It's something that's contagious and spreads, a particular universal, not an abstraction. It's very real, that one is precious and that one mediates a precious something, a precious feeling, an immediate sense that everyone is precious. I guess that is part of my unconscious ethics, the sense that one thing we should be doing is mediating for each other how precious we really are and acting from that and through that. The story of my grandfather being a rich man with my picture under his pillow, new life in the new country, I guess it's something that seeps deep in my unconscious, deeper than my personality and deeper than my problems in terms of conflicts with my bad self image. It is part of the richness of life. A pervasive caring, a positive aspect of boundaries, or lack of boundaries. No boundaries in that this feeling applies to everyone; boundaries because each person is approached in a special way.

Aner: Can you tell me more about your mother?

Mike: She was the first-born of three sisters and one brother. She was a gentle and caring person, at ease with people. As a couple, my parents could be called pretty old-fashioned, he more fierce and nervous, she softer and steadier. She and her siblings were good children, good adults, hard working, caring, and poor (laughs). They were simple folk. She and her brother were softer, her two sisters were jumpier, nervous, on the go. I grew up in a world of more or less simple people in an old-fashioned way. Even my father, who went to law school, was simple. His ego showed more than my mother's. She didn't yell. Interacting with her was rarely abrasive. The few times she erupted were monumental, throwing dishes, pots, furniture, screaming with frustrated rage at my father for God knows what, his drinking, probably, or issues I knew nothing of. When I was older she feared his behaviour would alienate me and I'd want nothing to do with them. As a young adult, that pretty much happened. Something in me did cut off from them, although a sense of closeness remained.

She was always doing for my father, doing for the family, for others. Fury caught up with her every half dozen years and she exploded. Perhaps it was exasperation with frustrating elements in her life that blew up. She was a very patient person, persistent (my father was impatient and persistent), up early, getting the house ready for the day, driving my father where he needed to go, for many years working in his office and learning law, preparing dinner. I did not think she was a particularly good cook and hated her eggs. She was famous for thick soups with meat bones and I never liked them either. I loved matzah-bry during Passover. She liked to serve fresh, unadorned vegetables, which I found tasteless but appreciate now. I understood at the time my feeling about her food was also about her. Goodness was there, caring was there, reliability was there, but something was missing.

She was also athletic, a swimmer and tennis player. She liked work. She wanted to teach mathematics but in her time there was a bias against women in mathematics. While in her teens she became an English and history teacher in high school, teaching kids just about her own age. I remember looking at Shakespeare projects her students did and sometimes I went with her to her school. I remember thinking the principal of the school looked like a whale and may have said so, a big red whale. I wondered at the strong impression—where did it come from?—to see someone that way. I felt a kind of marvel or thrill at this capacity. I must have been about three.

My mother was a good person, a helpful person. She wished people well and tried to help. She had spark and intelligence. But she never recovered after my brother died. It was not possible to digest what happened—digest is the wrong word. That God could do such things, that God would do this to her—it was not something she deserved, not something that was possible.

She told stories about visiting her grandmother in New York when she was a girl, taking the train, the bus, finding the tenement house, going up the stairs, spending the day with her Grandma, taking the ferry back. She was proud she did this all by herself and happy to be with Grandma. I can feel the sensuousness of the staircase, the candles, the salt air, the sweetness. She conveyed the warmth of the era, the close ties of caring people whom life treated harshly. She was in life. Not a loud life. A soft-spoken life with intolerable crashes. Even after she died inside when my brother died, she remained in life, part of life with people until near the end.

Aner: Now you live in Brooklyn, not far from where your mother visited her grandmother.

Mike: I came here to raise a family. My children are glad they lived here, although they are off now living their own lives. There is a lot of old life in Brooklyn, a good place for me. It's good to see all the young people coming in too.

There was something in my mother like a quiet bell, a soft, true ring. A kind of optimism, expecting people to be good, expecting herself to be good, expecting life to be good. It somehow did not make sense when life was bad, when people were bad. That's not the way it was supposed to be. They should be fixable and made right. There was always the sense that when things went wrong, they can be made right. But you cannot make the death of a child right.

Aner: In one of your books you describe how much your mother hurt you when you were a baby.

Mike: My mother was supportive and caring. Nevertheless, I felt terribly hurt by her going to work when I was very young, about eight months old. Child-caring thrilled, frightened, and stifled her. She needed to get out of the house to be herself another way. Maybe she was a bit ahead of her time, conflicted between self-sacrifice and autonomy, living both sides without reconciling them very well. A difficult task any time.

I was already two or three when I pretended not to mind when she left in the morning for work. She would say, "What a big boy." Meaning: "He doesn't mind that I'm leaving." I would steel myself to provide her with that impression. I felt like crying and fought against my tears. I made believe I was playing with my toys and didn't mind when she kissed me or waved and said, "Bye-bye." I can feel a contraction, a stiffening, as well as sobbing inside that goes on and on. A few years later she would call me "sour-puss", and asked why I didn't smile and was surprised to learn from other mothers that I smiled a lot away from home.

There is more I am afraid to say because it sounds crazy or impossible. I still feel the rip of her leaving to go to work when I was eight months old. The feeling that she couldn't (didn't want to) be with me and had to get away, the suffocated feeling she was escaping, and the tear through my body. My bearing it, hardening, making do. I learned to tell time in my crib, putting together the hands of a clock in my field of vision with morning radio shows. I remember—or imagine I remember—the eureka of matrices coming together and realizing the time the talk show host announced dovetailed with the position of the hands and numbers of the clock.

Aner: You connected the voice to the actual clock when you were less then a year old?

Mike: The visual sight with the radio voice. (Imitates) "Now it is Nine O Five, time for the Breakfast Show. Now it is Nine-fifteen, time to march around the breakfast table . . . Now it is Nine-thirty, time to . . ."

My rational thinking tells me that I had to be older than eight months of age. Maybe a year, or a year and a half? Yet my life feeling, my life memory tells me it was earlier.

Aner: Why were you so preoccupied with the clock at that age?

Mike: It was a recurrence, a correlation, a connection. I was very bright, in some ways one of those precocious ego developments Winniccott talks about. Nothing is simple though. Thinking was going on, feeling was going on. There probably are factors of historical time, class, culture. I give it as an instance of interweaving of circumstance and drive. Clock, radio, mother's leaving and returning—all parts of an affective spatial–temporal emotional, cognitive field that clicked together. I suppose the radio voice was a kind of mother. You piece together what you can with materials at hand. Radio was part of my life until I left for college. Later, as a teen, I listened to jazz when I went to sleep, and the jazz host told the time. Now I listen to news a lot and classical music. Still mothering myself, not always in good ways.

From my earliest writings on, you will find paragraphs sprinkled here and there that have analyses of time experience. An early paper collected in *The Electrified Tightrope*—"The recoil on having another person"—relates moving towards or away from the other to time experience. In the same book, there is a chapter on breathing and time experience. I've written on dream and time experience as well, on the feeling of time, love of time experience, a kind of wonder. The birth of clock time in my early childhood or infancy grew out of trauma time, providing an external frame of reference for acute agony, outside time to organize inside time, primal emotional time / timelessness.

You could call this coming together a taste of Bion's movement from insecurity and fragmentation to security and wholeness, his description of a rhythm in psychoanalytic sessions. You can also fit it with Lacan's descriptions of mastery masking trauma: how a gestalt provides a sense of unity when one's existential plight is otherwise. It arouses a profound awareness of things being connected, coming together, making sense. A deep underpinning of waiting in chaos with a sense that something illuminating, lifting, is about to happen. Such moments create a love of learning that has very deep roots. Psychoanalysis bears witness to love of insight in face of and growing out of trauma. The coming together of sound and sight in the telling of time was amazing in its own right but it had the extra dividend of defining the hours my mother would be away. She worked half a day and I knew, more or less, when she would return: I could tell [the] time.

My experience teaches me that there is something self-deluding about too facile an attitude about maternal going and coming. Some say, or perhaps wish, that a working mother is good for the baby, some say that staying at home is better. These are not easy issues and I am not sure there are satisfactory solutions. One does what one must in life but that does not make it good. Usually it's good this way, bad that way, unless it's just bad. There is a strong push to wish injury away. But one can't wish injury away. One doesn't stop living because of this, but at least we don't have to pretend we are not hurting each other.

It is one of the great aporias in life that a devoted parent can be so hurtful. An intricate mixture of self-giving, self-assertion, nourishment and injury. Emotional life challenges us.

Aner: Many mothers leave their babies and go to work. It doesn't have to be so traumatic.

Mike: I'm not sure about that any more. I don't know. I am not going to decide that. When you open things up and get to levels where pain is, other stories come out. I am not convinced by research on this topic. Often it sounds like rationalization of ideology, hopes, and wishes. I think it is important not to make believe that we know what is going on inside each other or inside an infant or a child. We interpret and speculate and construct. Sometimes we hit on a way of seeing and formulating that opens something up. We shouldn't be too smug about conceptions..

Aner: But mothers go to work on the assumption that it is not harmful to their children's well-being.

Mike: People do what they want to do and what they need to do. But we don't know the effects. When we see the spread of ADD and hyperactive disturbances and autism I think we [had] better reserve judgement and take each instance on its merit. I think my parents had a need to protect me from injury they inflicted. There are levels of protectiveness and reparation parents undertake, almost as attempts to mitigate harm they cause but feel helpless to avoid. Much of this is unconscious, but not all. A lot happens in semi-conscious, semi-unconscious ways. We are great self-justifiers and self-blamers no matter what we do. But neither blaming nor justifying gets to the realities of the case—they buzz around or cushion emotional facts. Something else is needed.

Aner: Who took care of you when your mother was out?

Mike: A young woman, maybe teenager, who was crazily scary. When my parents went out at night she would put cream on her face for her pimples, cover herself with a sheet, say she was a ghost and that she was going to kill my parents and I'd never see them again. We also spent time hiding in closets because she was afraid of people who came to the apartment door. I complained to my parents but they did not listen. At first I thought they didn't believe me because of my good imagination. As time went on I thought it more likely it was convenient for them to have her. She made things easier for them.

There is much adult insensitivity to childhood pain. Times have changed and people are more sophisticated but they do what's convenient and rationalize it. I give many examples in *Toxic Nourishment* and *Damaged Bonds*. Writing about my patients is also writing about myself. There are differences, of course. Sometimes I write about very busy and important or self-important or self-focused parents, not ill-meaning but insensitive in ways that matter. Without realizing it, they inflict injury that expresses their own unassimilated trauma history with new twists. That my parents did not listen now seems to me part of their own trauma history, insensitivity they endured in growing up and surviving. We are, in part, injury carriers, injury machines, pushing past something blood-curdling in our innards in order to live.

I begged my parents to fire this woman, who finally quit for reasons of her own when we moved from an apartment downtown to a house in a residential neighbourhood. By then I was five or six. I was so relieved when she left. I was happy to be free of her, but smouldering with anger and fear that I endured all those years, angry that my parents did not fire her. A few years later, I would set fire to the woods, not knowing why. It took many years to begin to recognize her as expressive of something in my parents, something gnarled, wounded, not only an exterior aberration.

The fact that I was not listened to about her added to my sense of isolation. Helpless fear, rage, clotted bad feeling, sick feeling. I had a deep sense of not being taken seriously, in spite of their care and devotion and love. Listening became a theme in my adult life. I've spent my life listening to others, keenly aware I am listening to myself as well, that the other is me, that we are working with damage we share and inflict. My writing is a kind of listening as well as a longing to be heard. I've been touched to find my voice touches others who need it. They hear the wound the writing comes from. A voice for those not listened to, a voice for the damage.

Aner: Why didn't they listen?

Mike: For a time I rationalized it as class and culture and historical time. Immigrants doing all they could to survive. Listening to feelings was not a high priority. You have to ignore an awful lot to get through. My feelings happened to be one thing they ignored. What was essential for me was not essential for them. But the truth is, I don't know. I don't know answers to many of your questions, but share my responses. My parents and I grew up in different worlds, with different interests, customs. Between me and them was a generation gap, a time and culture gap. I was the first in my family for whom English was the native language.

I felt my mother listened more than my father, at least provided the illusion or sense that she did. It was not that she heard or knew me, but that she cared, she loved. Mother love has a kind of biological specificity with a generic psychological template of sorts. Its specificity is part of its generic nature. Yet the specific person the mother bears, the who of the subject, me—may not be experienced or known as such. My baby, my child, this baby, this child. But the psychospiritual make-up of this child, my child, may elude the mother's grasp. The special contribution the child has to make in his or her own right may be off the mother's map. A mother may or may not understand (and understanding is variable: more, less, with different qualities) what sort of child is developing. A mother may care for and have the child's interest at heart. But what life feels like or is like for the child as an experiencing individual may not be something the mother can bear or take in or process. My meaning for a mother is not what life means for me. She may not have a clue as to what life is like for me. She may not be able to bear it.

Aner: It may be a mother cannot bear how awful things are for a child.

Mike: Yes, she needs to think things are better. I don't think my mother could experience my tormented nature, or maybe she did not know what to do with such agonized awareness. She had to think that things were better—good. How can a mother bear the unhappiness of a child—yet that is a task of motherhood. My mother was a good person and needed to feel I was a good person, and perhaps I was, to an extent. But how awful life could be was not something she wanted to know that I knew. Perhaps it was something she feared to know herself.

Aner: The mere fact that the child is not happy was not enough.

Mike: Happiness was not something that counted in many situations. Whether one was happy or not was not the main thing. You did what was necessary. They saw I was alive—I survived the horrors of my maid, so maybe it wasn't as horrible as I made out. I looked OK, acted OK enough as far as they were concerned. I was bright and lively and interested in everything. People looked at me with satisfaction. You do what you need to do, what life allows. They put up with pain and hardship. One of life's aporias: parents wanting life to be better or happier for their children, while transmitting their traumatized selves, passing pain, deformation and self-hardening on. To want life to be easier, happier—but how? How can you make life easy? Are you asking the wrong thing of life?

My father thought in material terms. My mother was aware of emotional needs but in global, non-specific ways. They did not have many categories for nuances of psychic pain. I think they were out of their depth when it came to the emotional life of babies or themselves.

Aner: I suspect many people are rather helpless in face of what emotional life exacts.

Mike: Yes, My parents winged it as best they could and hoped it would come out all right. They lacked capacity to know how bad things were for me emotionally and there was nothing they could do if they knew. I spent many years learning how to be with my torment. I now know many do. It takes a special development to be sensitive to psychic pain and use that sensitivity well. A lot of unconscious insensitivity is the rule. But often there is latent awareness that we are not doing ourselves justice.

Adults in my life were sensitive and feeling. Affect was in the air. But it was not a sensitivity or feeling that makes a child's feelings visible or palpable. It was feeling and sensitivity unto itself, atmospheric. In my father's case, self-centred, in my mother's, self-giving. It was sort of an emotional atmosphere without a sense of a child's subjectivity. The result felt like two trees in the middle of my garden, one without nerve-endings, the other with a rich supply of nerve endings and, with Schreber, soul was in the nerves.

A stake through the garden's heart: my father saying when I was in pain, "What you feel when you're a child doesn't matter. What happens when you're grown up is what counts." An insensitive bar in the middle of emotional being.

Aner: What happens to trust when emotionality is conjoined with inability to respond to another's subjective being?

Mike: Trust doesn't die but personality twists to preserve it in idiosyncratic ways. My father even said, "Children don't have feelings." Does this mean children don't exist or count? Not exactly, children count an infinite lot, but what children feel does not count.

Who or what is this infinitely precious being, loved by devoted parents, supposed not to have subjective existence of his or her own, infinitely precious without feelings that count? "You are young now, you are just a baby, and your feelings don't matter. When you get older you'll see what counts." Words break bones that don't exist in spatial reality.

So much goes on outside parental radar, outside parental ability to perceive or process, and survives secretly in ruin as rigidity, contraction, debris. Perhaps secret is not the right word. But humans have come up with the idea of keeping secrets from themselves, self as special secret.

As I suggested earlier, my father was horrified later in life when I brought up such remarks. He couldn't believe he said them and shed tears over [the] pain his personality caused those dearest to him, and glimpsed the pain his personality caused himself as well. He prematurely became adult and discounted the slow, wayward processes of childhood. At the same time, self-indulgent egoism escaped self-criticism and poured into his children. My mother was more receptive, but lacked sensors for the kinds of hells that opened in me. She pacified, bypassed, smoothed over, hoping life would be normal.

I learned there were feelings you were stuck with. There is no way to communicate them. From an early age I was conscious of subjective life that had no place to go. Is that why I write so many books? Finally, I've found places?

Aner: Is that how they treated their own selves?

Mike: Yes, there is nothing to complain about. You get on with it. You do what you have to do. Life's tasks. You have a child, a joy; you have family, a joy. There is no need to know the pain inside. What could you do with it anyway? The day is enough to get through.

Aner: Were your parents physical persons? Did they love to hug and kiss you?

Mike: My father was more physical with affection than my mother. She was more reserved, had more boundaries, less at ease with hugs and physicality. My father was huggy, couldn't keep his hands off. He also kissed. He wanted to kiss mouth to mouth. I backed off from this at a young age. Someone told me it was part of his culture in the old country, males kissing mouth to mouth. My mother was more American in some ways. My father was a very worried person. I think she masked her anxiety with calm. She was the soother in the family. Many years later I realized that she was fearful, too. Her anxiety came into the open after my father died. I think he lived it out for her and when he died she was alone with no one to soothe.

My mother was nourished by being with others. She loved family gatherings. I do not think she ever missed a family event. I never was comfortable with family gatherings.

Aner: Why?

Mike: People at family gatherings seemed more of a piece. It was difficult to fit myself into being a version of a person they might recognize. I learned how to do this better later. I became more adept at choosing ways to act that met the situation, more or less.

I've always been aware of emotions for which conversation lacked room. I suspect many people are, but people in my life did not seem troubled by this. How do you fit loose parts of yourself in? Jiggle yourself together somehow?

I've always felt difficulty stuffing the looseness of self into packages for social contact. Therapy sessions provided a place where interesting kinds of contact were possible outside the boxes. I was sensitive to alternate states and avenues of contact from a very early age. Dreams and images always were important to me and I thought about them with wonder and hunger. Later, when I heard the Talmudic saying that an uninterpreted dream was like an unopened letter from God, I realized that the contact dreams offered touched something very special. Digging into dreams was like digging into secret life. Buried treasure. Secret and sacred. A penetrating sense of mystery that is part of self and life. Sensuous, sexual, spiritual—parts of precious mystery.

I played sexual games with girl cousins at family gatherings. When we were young, people thought nothing of us rolling around the floor. I guess they ignored what we were trying to do. We sometimes partly succeeded [in] pressing pleasure buttons, although I felt guilty for instigating these activities. Years later one of my cousins reminded me of what fun we had doing that, and I realized she liked it too.

When I was older, I felt vaginal sensation open to light in psychospiritual vision and in sexual intercourse. I was in love with symbolic meaning long before I knew it. My chapter, "Alone with God", in *The Sensitive Self*, depicts how a profound God-sense can arise in a person who needs contact in secret deep places. The woman I wrote about knew tormented aloneness, although she grew up in a very social milieu. She did not know what to do with sensitivity in a world of tough, kindly adults largely blind to what a child might feel.

Aner: It seems that you developed a sensitivity that was rare in your surroundings.

Mike: I don't know to this day why I am so different, not only from my family but from the milieu I was part of. Many I grew up with are living good lives in New Jersey. I had an ear for pain. As I grew older, I became aware [that] people talked out their sufferings with me; people in crises came to see me. I had a feel for suffering, not in the sense that I was big-hearted or empathic or very feeling, but that I could and would listen to anything. There was nothing people couldn't tell me. I loved hearing it all—every nook and cranny, every weed. I felt I was learning about life. When I read, it was to hear truth about life, to taste wisdom. I wanted to know what was inside people, every bit of us. I can listen to people all day, although I dip in and out. I just like hearing it. I think of Errol Garner, a self-taught jazz pianist who couldn't read music but could play any song in any key. When asked how he did it, he would say something like, well, how do you breathe or have sex. It's just something I do, listening and writing. It's what comes naturally. I also like to talk and that is why I teach—to see what will come out of me if I let go. It's a necessary outlet.

Aner: I suspect part of the background for this kind of activity has to do with being alone a lot in early childhood.

Mike: That is not an adequate explanation, but it is a factor. I spent my first five years or so in a neighbourhood where there weren't kids my age. I was very lonely and made up imaginary playmates, and one of my favourite songs I heard on the radio was "Come Play with Me", or maybe it was called "Playmates". As luck would have it, my father heard about a boy my age falling out of his apartment window to his death. We lived on the fifth or sixth floor of an apartment building in downtown Passaic at the time. Within months he bought a house (for $3000) in a residential neighbourhood and I had my own room and plenty of kids my age to play with.

My whole life changed. A kid came up to me, introduced himself, and I was happy and jumping with feelings and said: "Would you teach me how to play?" From that point (I was about six years old) I was outdoors all hours with the kids. Aloneness didn't stop: I rode my bike by myself all over Passaic and adjoining towns and country. I liked going places myself. The deep alone feeling, the quiet: I love it. Now I had both: friends to play with and myself alone.

Getting my father to get me a bike wasn't an easy thing. He was afraid I'd get killed. In fact my brother got killed the way my father feared I would. Every year he'd promise to get me the bike, then find reasons not to. For several years he swore there wasn't enough metal to make bikes because of the war effort. I learned about broken promises. One residue is I never made a promise I couldn't keep. I rarely, if ever, make promises at all (actually, I can't remember ever making a promise). I marvel at people who are loose enough to take their word with a grain of salt and don't feel bound by it. I doubt if I could handle politics. I've had to learn to loosen up and not take myself or others so seriously. One of the things I'm proud of: a patient who read my work remarked that it does not convey how funny I am. I'm not proud that my writing fails in this regard, but I'm happy my patient felt like this about me.

Another thing about me as a youngster—I would befriend kids others made fun of. I was appalled by childhood ridicule, that kids made kids suffer so. There was enough pain from parents. It didn't yet dawn on me that life was inherently painful, that categories like adult or child did not limit awfulness. I was not a clique person. My friends spanned categories, working and middle class (I knew very few uppers), different ethnic and national backgrounds, different kinds of personalities and interests, including those left out. I liked being part of different worlds. It made life richer. I don't think I was rejected by any of the groups, but I didn't become wholly part of any either. I remained somewhat outside the various systems I took part in.

CHAPTER THREE

Supervision

First supervision: love affair

*A*ner: Rahel is a married woman, age forty-five. She is a mother to three children from her second marriage. Rahel is in therapy for five years. She comes twice a week on a regular basis. Rahel first came to therapy, seven years ago, because she felt depressed. She cried a lot, felt miserable and barely functioned in her work as a secretary. Rahel also suffered from a compulsion to wash her hands, put them under the tap for several minutes, especially before cooking or after washing the house with detergents. She feared that residues of detergents remaining on her hands might mix with cooked food and poison her family.

Mike: How long has Rahel been married?

Aner: Rahel married when she was twenty-three. She is a small woman. She has a child look. It is hard to believe that she is forty-five. Rahel suffered many catastrophes. Her mother died from a car accident when she was nine. She was sent abroad and was raised by her uncle until the age of seventeen. She returned to Israel when her father had a stroke. Her father died three years later. Before his death Rahel had to take care of him. For years she felt guilty because of her parents' deaths. She was in the kitchen with her mother a few days before the car accident. Rahel's mother was cooking and washing the dishes in the kitchen. Suddenly an unpleasant thought "jumped" into Rahel's mind: how great it would be if she could replace her mother in the kitchen. After her mother's death she thought her private thought might have caused the death. She was tormented by guilt feelings. Her memories of her mother are ambivalent. Her mother was not warm or affectionate.

Rahel felt close to her father. He often visited her when she was abroad with her uncle and his wife. They had daily conversations on the phone. He supported her financially. He told her how he liked her look, complimented her about her talents. When he got sick Rahel took care of him like a little woman. She cooked, cleaned, and nursed him. After he died she thought she could have prevented his death if she was more devoted and caring. If only she prepared better food for him, or took him to the doctors more often, she might have saved his life. For years she felt depressed and guilty. Rahel had a young brother who had been schizophrenic since her adolescence. He spent most of his life in a psychiatric hospital. After a few weeks in therapy Rahel made good progress and there was an enormous relief in her symptoms.

Mike: How did you do that?

Aner: I don't know. It just happened. I guess it was something in our relationship, a movement, a quiet happening, a blessing. It was really amazing.

But then Rahel began to complain about her mother-in-law. These complaints were more resistant to therapy. She repeated them in almost every session. She felt that her mother-in-law did not welcome her to the family. She felt rejected by her mother-in-law. She thought her mother-in-law wished and prayed for "bad things" to happen to her. According to Rahel, these bad wishes and prayers influenced her life in a profound and tragic way. She thinks her whole miserable situation is because of her mother-in-law's bad spell.

Mike: How often do they see each other?

Aner: In Israel family ties are very close. They meet very often. The year of crisis between her and her mother-in-law began after she gave birth to her first child. After the birth her husband put a

lot of pressure on her to stay with his family, and she agreed reluc-
tantly. She had some kind of after birth depression, I am not sure
how severe it was, but apparently her mother-in-law questioned
her ability to be a mother and, according to my patient, refused to
help her. The husband's family was in distress. They asked for
professional help from the welfare services. A social worker was
sent. My patient felt humiliated. For Rahel it was a traumatic experience. In some sessions she repeats again and again the same story
in the same words. She felt awful.

Mike: Why does she think the mother-in-law is against her?

Aner: Rahel thinks her mother-in-law thinks she owns the son and
that she refuses to let go of him. They are competing for the same
man, only they are not equal. Her mother-in-law is powerful and
bad, her prayers are heard somewhere but Rahel feels weak and
helpless.

Mike: What position does the son/husband take?

Aner: The son is a *Nebech*. He is a passive and weak; anger and
conflicts intimidate him. He just wants things to be quiet between
the two.

Mike: Isn't it strange that such a passive man has two women
fighting about him?

Aner: Yes. He is trying to negotiate between the two. He keeps
saying that Rahel sees elephants where there are only flies. Frankly,
I don't really know what's going on because Rahel can make false
attributions, like her conviction that her mother-in-law's "bad
thoughts" had a devastating effect on her life.

Mike: Did Rahel say more about that?

Aner: Well, at first she was ashamed to tell me. Rahel is not
psychotic, but she can be paranoid. It's a cultural thing. She knows
exactly how it sounds from the outside. She doesn't have a clear
idea how these things work.

Mike: What bad things have happened so far?

Aner: She got fired. She has been unemployed for a couple of
years and she thinks her mother-in-law has something to do with

it. As long as that woman wishes her misfortune the world cannot be a safe place.

Mike: Is there any other motive besides the competition with her son that Rahel attributes to her mother-in-law?

Aner: Yes. Rahel thinks her mother-in-law, whom she likes to call "primitive", envies her attractive appearance and modernity. Rahel feels her mother-in-law wishes my patient to be exactly like her: primitive, arrange her life around household duties, neglect her physical appearance.

Mike: What more can you tell me about Rahel?

Aner: She doesn't have any friends. She doesn't like or appreciate women very much. When Rahel did work, she did not get on with the other female workers. Rahel thought that they didn't like her for two reasons: First, she was prettier; second, the boss preferred her. There is always a strong powerful woman that turns against her, cursing her secretly and thinking bad thoughts. Likewise, there is always a good-looking nice man who treats her nicely and favours her. In her work it was her boss. She felt there was something special between them. Rahel thinks the other women envied her special relations with her boss. The man is always weak compared to some powerful woman who wants to take him away from her. But no matter how strong the powerful woman is, she is always inferior to Rahel because she lacks Rahel's beauty and attractiveness. A few weeks before she was fired, she thought that one of the female workers tried to poison her by putting deadly pills in her tea. She was embarrassed to tell me that because she was not sure if I would believe her. She did not want me to think that she is mad.

Before her marriage a young educated man fell in love with Rahel and wanted to marry her. Rahel remembers that he was fond of her. She proudly describes how she attracted him and how he liked to smell her body and touch her. She misses him and often has daydreams about what would have happened if she lived with him. Eventually, Rahel didn't marry him because she thought that his family would never accept an uneducated and simple woman like her.

Mike: Tell me more about the therapy.

Aner: From the beginning Rahel felt aroused and tensed in my presence. Our relations became very lively. After the first two years, just after she got out of her depression, she was convinced I was desperately in love with her. For her our relationship was a love affair. She thought we must keep it in secret. Before sessions she did not put on her make-up so her husband wouldn't suspect that anything fishy was happening between us. She asked me if I love my wife. She added that she wouldn't dream of taking her place. Though she felt we were having an affair, she was certain that I loved my wife deeply and would never give her up. In one dramatic session she came to my office and noticed the wires coming out of my computer. She asked me if my wife had installed a recording device so she could listen to our conversations. She is certain that I am afraid of our relationship, that I can't handle it, that it is too much for me.

Mike: What do you tell her?

Aner: I always feel that Rahel is distorting what I say. It is as if she hears whatever she wants to. If I say A, she understands B. Now B is always something against her, a criticism. For example if I say: "It was hard for you to realize that your mother-in-law would not welcome you to her family", she answers: "No, I am not a miserable woman", or: "It's not only in my head", or: "It's not just me, every woman who marries her husband needs to feel welcomed and accepted by her mother-in-law". Whatever I would say, Rahel would feel that I attacked or criticized her. She is also extremely demanding. She wants to know if I really love her and then says she is certain that I love my wife and not her. Sometimes it's hard to bear her. I feel that she wants so much and that she feels I give her so little. Rahel pays me a ridiculously low fee because she is unemployed. Yet she is insulted by the mere fact that she has to pay me. At some meetings Rahel says she won't come next week because she doesn't have enough to pay me. Then she adds: "You wouldn't consider giving me a discount, would you?" I tell her that she is testing me. If I really loved her I would reduce her fee, perhaps even agree to meet her for free. But what she really wants to hear is that I really want her to come. "It is important that you come", I tell her. "You feel so lonely and have no one to talk to. It's not a good idea to skip a session." Rahel enjoys seeing how I work hard for her to change her mind. It's like a ritual in which everyone has to play his part: She says she won't come, I sweat blood to convince her. The drama ends when she finally succumbs and agrees. Sometimes she says: "It's important for me to come, but what about you?" When I tell her that it will make me happy to see her next week she blushes and hides a little smile.

Mike   Do you spend extra time with Rahel?

Aner: No, fifty minutes are enough and sometimes too much.

Mike: Does Rahel miss appointments?

Aner: Never. She comes even when she is sick.

Mike: How do you like Rahel?

Aner: Rahel is special for me despite the difficulties. It feels good to nurture someone who is extremely deprived but is willing to be nurtured. Rahel never had such an experience—being the centre of a relationship. But, as you can see, she is not an easy patient. I often think of her as ungrateful. Whatever I give her, whatever I do for her, it's just not enough.

On the other hand, I feel that Rahel is afraid of getting too close to me. She keeps saying that I limit her by saying that my relationship with her is purely professional. I never said that. In reality she is the one who feels very tense and shy in my presence. She once told me that it embarrasses her to drink water or do any thing with her body in my presence. She told me she would like to be more spontaneous and less reserved when we sit together. She says that if she could just take her shoes off in my presence, or jump, or do silly things like a child it will make her feel good. In many sessions she expresses an urge to see me more. She says she misses me, that fifty-minute sessions are not enough. She wants us to spend more time together. But of course she says, insulted, "You won't agree to see me free of charge, would you?" And, of course, she continues," I wouldn't expect you to." It is always me who rejects her, because I live without her.

Mike: If you would want Rahel enough, what would happen then?

Aner: I don't know. Sometimes I ask myself if Rahel heard me at all. I want to shout: hello, do you hear what I just said? Rahel keeps twisting things as though I am criticizing her and she has to defend herself.

Mike: What stops Rahel from feeling how special she is for you?

Aner: Maybe I'm missing something here.

Mike: Ask her: Rahel, what makes you deaf to what I am saying? What stops you from hearing me? How do you do that? How does that happen?

She is protecting herself. Maybe over time it is possible to explore what that is. How do you do that? What is it that is doing that? What protects you from yourself? How does that work that you are so good at shutting me out?

Aner: Are you saying that I should confront her?

Mike: No, not confront; raise it and bring it up. I wouldn't necessarily expect Rahel to answer or to be able to answer, but at least plant seeds for the future. Why do you think there is such an enormous force, and what is this force you experience as not hearing?

Aner: I am not sure what it is that Rahel doesn't want to hear.

Mike: Rahel doesn't know what to do with the other's good feelings. Maybe she thinks: as soon as I have good feelings I'll die, or the therapy will have to stop. You can suggest that to her: maybe you are afraid that if good feelings happen the therapy will have to end.

Look what happened with her closest bonds as she grew up. Something good signals a catastrophe is on the way, so she has to protect herself from the depth of a bond. Bonds end up catastrophically, with death and madness, or jealousy. Destructive forces kick into gear once feelings start. Love means catastrophe, bond means catastrophe, feelings mean catastrophe, anything close or significant means death or madness: my brother went crazy, my mother died, my father died. That's quite a background. Rahel is doing very well. Rahel has a right to be insane. She has a psychotic part. I wouldn't expect too much sanity.

How did Rahel feel about her brother's insanity?

Aner: She was ashamed of his illness. She was also afraid that she will be ill too.

Mike: Her whole nuclear family died?

Aner: She doesn't have anyone except her mother's brother. But she is disappointed with him too.

Mike: So Rahel has to protect herself, she is very self protective. Seeing the other as bad is a way of protecting herself. Sometimes she is right and the other *is* bad. Other times her sense that bonds can be catastrophic spreads and she tries to contain the spread by focusing on specific target figures. It is a battle between spreading catastrophe and focused catastrophe. Why wouldn't Rahel lose her husband and children if she lost everyone else? So the rituals are protective and also show how Rahel feels responsible for her losses. Rahel is afraid that those she loves will be taken away from her. She thinks inside herself: if only I can be good enough, clean enough, pure enough, God won't take them from me. Rahel is afraid her mother-in-law will take you away from her. Her mother-in-law's magic and brutal powers will steal you away.

Aner: Fortunately, we don't know each other.

Mike: It doesn't matter. You don't have to know each other in order for bad magic power to work. You don't have to be near each other. What distance can bad power travel? How far away can badness or evil intentionality or unconscious negative magical force be and still be effective? Does bad power only work when there is literal contact or can it work at a distance too? Bad power can traverse immense distances instantaneously. It can travel from mind to mind, body to body without barriers. Rahel feels there is a bad force in the universe that is working against her and she has to try to defend herself against it. In so far as you are a good force, Rahel has to protect you too.

Aner: If there is one area that the powerful mother-in-law has not touched, it is the therapeutic relation. Until you said that I felt quite safe.

Mike: (laughs). So far Rahel kept the bad force somewhat circumscribed. She tells the bad force: you can have this area but not that area. Rahel is afraid that the bad force will go further and take her children, her husband, and will stop therapy.

Aner: She was scared that she will become mad, too, like her brother.

Mike: Yes. I'd like to hear more about that.

Aner: It does not concern her now as much as it did. But when Rahel was depressed she thought she was going mad. She wanted me to reassure her that she is OK, which I did. She refused to take psychiatric treatments to relieve her depression and compulsion. Her brother took medication and other psychiatric treatments all his life. Rahel could not bear the thought that they share the same fate. She did not want to end up like her brother.

Mike: Tell me more about the therapeutic process.

Aner: After a session in which Rahel feels close to me, I can almost anticipate the next session. In it she would describe again her compulsive hand-washings. In the libidinal session she might say:" I know you would never choose a woman like me, I am not the kind of woman you are interested in, but I must tell you, I really think of you a lot, I imagine us doing things together." And then she will add that she would rather not discuss it right now. Then comes the next session when she focuses on her symptoms: Will this come to an end? Can you help me more then you have already done? In contrast to the previous session she will not mention anything personal. It is as if she is trying to clean the "sins" of the previous sessions.

Mike: They are connected. Rahel is saying that if I have strong feelings for you, you will be taken away from me. No matter how much I wash my hands it's not enough to protect you from bad forces.

There's no end to washing bad or good or strong feelings away, feelings that I'm afraid of, feelings that disturb me. One never stops trying to wash them away. To wash is to clean but also to get rid of. To wash one's hands of something means to drop the matter, to no longer be interested, to let something go, get rid of it, let it fall, drop it out of one's life. A little like sending a scapegoat over a cliff. Get rid of sin, of disturbance, of problems. In America there is a song that says, "I'm going to wash that man right out of my hair". Which hair, you might wonder, top or bottom or both. Out of one's psychic hair. To wash the psyche clean and create a disturbance-free psyche.

Compulsive washing also defends against loss and damage, tries to undo loss and damage. When Rahel has good feelings or sexy feelings for you, they threaten the relationship. Because they are too much, too exciting, overwhelming, too good or too hot to handle, *and* because they are subject to loss, damage, attack, spoilage. They can be ruined and taken away. Rahel has to spoil her feelings so she can feel protected. She washes her hands so much when she cooks because she is afraid to poison the food with bad or disturbing or good or exciting feelings. Too much of her will run off into the food, too much spillage, drainage of her insides into the food. Rahel is really afraid. When she gets to the point of thinking, "They are laughing at me, they think I'm crazy", I would tell her, "You don't have to think it's [handwashing, etc.] sane. Just let it be. Maybe after therapy goes on for a while, it will make more sense. Part of the reason that you have to do this is because you are afraid of losing those who are close to you, so you try to purify yourself, so death won't happen again."

We try to wash sin away; we try to wash death away. We try to wash evil and madness away. We try to preserve ourselves and others by washing away what might infect us. Washing, too, is a kind of self-protective murder since it tries to kill off what is bothering one (psychic dis-ease). Rahel feels that if she doesn't do a good job as a mother and as a wife her family will be hurt and the same goes for you. She has to nurture and preserve her therapy against great odds.

Aner: In what way?

Mike: She has to nourish you *and* give you her pathology. In a way, it is like feeding a cancer. Rahel has to see that you stay alive and well in face of omnipresent danger. She has to help you survive and flourish in face of the sickness she puts into you. She has to find some way to feel good enough to stay in therapy, to be a wife, to be a mother, to be a patient, because she doesn't feel good enough.

For now, I wouldn't do too much with the mother-in-law. Her ideas about the mother-in-law are pretty fixed. I wouldn't attack them, I wouldn't try to solve them, I wouldn't invest too much on this front at this point. It's better at this stage to support her, reassure her, saying something like, "Oh, that was a lousy thing for your mother-in-law to say. I don't blame you for feeling that way."

That is, just acknowledge her feelings. To explore and investigate is likely to feel rejecting, unless she begins to hunger for such activity. Rahel is likely to use anything she learns to feel worse about herself. Right now she is less curious than frightened, trying to keep threat at bay. I wouldn't introduce the mother-in-law as a major focus unless she forces you to. I would stay with the things she does to protect the people she loves in her life, acknowledging that she is afraid something bad will happen to them. Look what's happened in the past; you fear you are going to lose those who are close to you; you are trying now to make things better. It's like biblical purification on a stationary bicycle. You keep pedalling and pedalling, trying to clean yourself enough so God will not do bad things, so those you love can go on living. What does one have to do to stop God from doing bad things?

Aner: It's a lot of self-blaming.

Mike: Rahel suffered enormous losses . . . She seems to be a fairly rich personality given what she has gone through.

Aner: You think so?

Mike: Don't you? She has feelings for you; she has all these crazy ideas. You are doing a good job.

Aner: It's good to hear you say that.

Mike: Rahel thinks that you are afraid to feel for her. She feels you should be afraid of your feelings or you will leave your wife. If you are not afraid of your feelings what will happen with the two of you? To have feelings means *too much* feelings. There is boundlessness at work, so she works so hard to keep things bounded. To have feelings means uncontrollable feelings, a flood, destructive gratification. Yet you sit with her and you show her that you have good feelings for her. Rahel and you are still with each other. You are managing to survive having feelings for each other. But there is always threat. Tell Rahel: You have a right to be afraid. You feel I am afraid of you and you are afraid of me. Why are you so afraid of that? Maybe that's how human beings are, afraid of each other. We don't know what to do with feelings. No one teaches us what to do. You are left in the forest or desert to take care of yourself. What do we do with the feelings we have? Maybe therapy is a place where over time something can happen. We can learn about feelings, become less afraid of some of our feelings. We can learn to dip in.

Aner: Rahel thinks of our relationship in a very rigid way. She thinks there are just two ways: either it is a professional relationship, nothing personal, she is just one of my patients; or it's a love relationship.

Mike: Did you point out this dichotomy, either everything or nothing?

Aner: Many times.

Mike: Isn't therapy strange? What relationships are like it? We talk about the most personal, intimate things. The therapist invites the patient to say anything and everything. Yet we are still therapist and patient. It is a weird relationship, a different kind of relationship. How is this relationship different from all other relationships? Why did human beings invent such a relationship? If they invented it, it must have a purpose; let's see if we can find out.

Aner: That's much too philosophical for her.

Mike: Then try asking: what do you make of this strange relationship, intimate yet not intimate, close but not close?

Aner: Rahel would answer: it's because of *you*. I want more of you but you insist that it's all professional.

Mike: But do you find that sometimes I am too close, and sometimes I am too far, that I don't get it just right? You are telling me that it is frustrating for you; it is aggravating that I don't get it right. Too close, too far, too cold, too warm. Maybe it takes time for us to learn how to be together.

Aner: I am not sure if Rahel could be at ease with this subject.

Mike: Let it stay unresolved. One lives with a lot that's unsolved. It takes a lot of patience, two people together.

Aner: For her, just talking about such things is a sin. This kind of talk is too intimate, verbal intercourse is sexual intercourse. She came to solve her problems not to have an affair. And yet she enjoys flirting with me.

Mike: The biggest problem that we are working with and hope to make a little better is the feeling that all the good things in your life will be taken away from you. Relationships mean catastrophe. Something catastrophic is going to happen. You think all the time while you are living that bad things will happen. You know you are not wrong. Bad things do happen and have happened and will happen. Now you want to go further. You want to live in spite of such knowledge. One thing I feel about the washing is that it is a place where you want to make things better. Can you say more about this feeling of trying to make things better?

Aner: Rahel feels that she doesn't cook enough and that her children complain about it. She does not experience herself as a fully nurturing mother. It's amazing how food is enormously important in some cultures. On the other hand, before Rahel worked she spent many hours in the kitchen like "a good mother" but she didn't like it. It was bad then, and it is bad now. Everything is bad, nothing is good. It's hard for her to acknowledge anything good in her life.

Mike: If she does it will be taken away. I can feel that there are some things you feel *are* good. You are afraid to acknowledge them, you are afraid to say them, you are afraid that they will be taken away. Only show the bad things. Keep all the good things secret because if someone sees them they will be taken away.

Aner: So for Rahel good means a pending catastrophe?

Mike: Yes. Lots of damage. The bad is a protective shield. If everything is going to be bad there is not too much of a loss.

Aner: I am worried; I don't see a movement there. I am not sure if change is possible.

Mike: Don't be. How long can she stay?

Aner: I don't see an end.

Mike: That's good. That means that she can stand it. Rahel senses something true in the relationship. Don't worry about change. It will happen by itself. It will happen through the interaction over time, a little here, a little there. I wouldn't look for big things. Just stay with Rahel and something will happen. It's already happening. Don't ask if this is going to go away, or if that's going to go away.

That's the wrong question. Just keep on going and see what will happen. There will be emotional change just from being together and going through things.

Aner: I always felt pessimistic about Rahel's life and optimistic about therapy. There is something in her therapy that goes very well and is good for her. But I don't see a similar rhythm in her life.

Mike: Therapy is life. Therapy is part of her life, a support, a background. It's a lot. For Rahel it is an interaction with an interesting man whom she can't have, who is too good for her (laughs), who is above her. Like the daddy she never had. For her you are someone who is interested, someone who looks for her.

Aner: Once a month we have an almost routine session in which she says that she must quit therapy otherwise she would get used to it and might never leave.

Mike: Rahel might feel that she has to leave because she must protect you from her destructiveness. Then you should say: if this therapy ends it's not because I am getting rid of you, it's because you are getting rid of me. I am here. I am sticking it out. I'll stick it out if you can take it. But you are the one who can't take it and has to go.

   If she has to go, make sure Rahel understands that she can come back at some point. Tell her not to let her shame stop her from coming back when she wants to. Give her an escape hatch and leave the door open. You understand she feels locked in by therapy and has to get away now.

Aner: I understand. I think you are saying that I feel locked in with Rahel and that I have to get away. Not any more. Being in a dyad with her is suffocating. But now you are in the picture. You hold both of us. That's liberating.

Mike: That's terrific. God bless you. A bond contains toxic and all kinds of negative elements. If you keep bearing it, things happen. Rahel has to keep purifying herself by washing her hands because she doesn't have an intersubjective washing, a soul washing, a psyche washing.

Aner: Surprisingly, Rahel's hand-washing has declined since I've been here in the States.

Mike: (laughs). You are here, she is there. You survive without her, she survives without you. It's less intense, she doesn't have to protect you as much. When you're together, she has to protect you more. Contact heats things up, is more intense, she has to protect you (and herself) more. Overall, you are communicating: "You are afraid for me and have to protect me with the washing. Our relationship will survive. You don't have to work so hard. Let it go." Your coming to the States, leaving her, is an act of faith, a letting go.

Aner: Some sessions are often structured like a drama with a beginning, a peak and an exciting finale. She opens the session talking about her symptoms and how awful she feels. She goes on to talk about us. She starts to get excited, smiles a lot as if she is playing and enjoying. At that phase she seems less tense. As the session ends she gets highly aroused. A few seconds before the session ends she wants to know how I feel about her.

Mike: (raises his voice): You waited for the very end of the hour to ask me the most important question on your mind? I want you to start next session with this question. I want you to practise asking that question earlier.

Aner: I am not sure. I don't feel comfortable saying that.

Mike: You don't have to be so serious. Come in and ask her: How do I look like I feel about you right now? Maybe each time it will be something different. Maybe I feel different things about you at different times. Next session when I ask you, you'll see something else.

The point here is to help her get some psychic exercise. Rahel gets stuck on one track. She has an imperative, a demand: You should feel one thing for me, whatever that one thing is at the moment, for example, passion and love. Thou shall feel passion and love. By asking, "How do I look like I feel towards you now? And now? And now?" you are creating a counter-demand, or invitation, or counter-current, making waves, creating the possibility of some undulating movement. "How do I look now? Is it the same as last time, is it different? What's the same? What's different?" Perhaps she will begin to exercise her psyche. A little like artificial respiration. You are trying to stimulate some movement between perceptions, without being too dogmatic or pushy. It is an extended invitation to move around a bit.

Aner: When she asks me that final dramatic question at the end—what feelings do I have for her?—I feel tension in the air. It's like the whole session was built to get to that point.

Mike: A work of art [raises his voice dramatically], all session you worked to get to this point, to ask me this question as you are walking out the door. That's awesome. How did you do that? Save the best for last. Then you don't need me any more.

Aner: I still don't know how to answer.

Mike: (amused). Oh, my God, now that you are leaving? How can I possibly say it all in thirty seconds? How do you think I feel? Next time ask me two minutes earlier.

Aner: That will be the wrong answer for her. I always give her the wrong answer. For her I should be saying: I love you as much as you love me. That's what Rahel expects me to say.

Mike: That's very nice. So say: I love you much as you love me. How do you feel saying that?

Aner: It's not true.

Mike: I have a psychotic patient who often says at the end of sessions, so, am I going to be OK? Am I going to be OK? Tell me I am going to be OK. Sometimes I answer: You will be OK. And he says: no, no, say it like you mean it, say Jay, you are going to be OK. Sometimes I do say, Jay, you will be OK.

I may have my doubts, my fears. I hope and pray he will be OK. In some sense, like a mother, I am conveying he is OK now. There is something lovable about him. He is a profoundly good person, profoundly troubled, in need, and I do care. When I say, "You are going to be OK, Jay", I feel skin form around him. It is quite a moving sensation, to mediate the growth of skin. A second before, it wasn't there, he was raw. He was asking to be in a body with skin, a psyche with skin. My holding back withheld the growth of skin. My giving enabled its formation. It changes one's picture of self and life to realize that words form skin.

You said before you told her Rahel would be OK but it is hard for you to say I love you? Aner, don't say something you are not comfortable with. Ask her: how do I look to you? What can you tell about my feelings when you look at my face?

Aner: She is very interested in finding how I *really* feel for her. I feel trapped. Whatever I say it's not the right answer.

Mike: You always have the right to reflect. The assumption is that you feel only one thing at a time for her. Rahel may see things in you that you don't want her to see. She may be right about you. She wishes for more or something else. Rahel wants you to love her more, to be more devoted to her, to want her the way she wants you. But you do have your own mind, or at least a mind somewhat independent of her mind. She fears giving her mind or your mind space. She wants to fill the space with one thing. One mind, one thing. Two minds, one thing. But a mind, yours or hers, contains other possibilities. Whatever pressure you feel, you have to keep in mind what a complex person you are. You have to keep on being a complex person no matter how simplified she wants to make things. There is a force at work to reduce complexity and you must withstand it. Rahel is afraid to see that she is not of one mind. She fears the loss of the love she hopes to have. Rahel does not think she can have a mind and love at the same time. She is not yet able to let love vary but something in her sees the handwriting on the wall and fights it.

Aner: For her it's a multiple choice, it's A or B.

Mike: If I won't feel the right thing, you won't like it, you will feel rejected. Maybe I feel some of the right thing, some of the wrong thing; some of this, some of that. I feel a mixture of things. But a mixture may not be enough.

I have nothing against saying, "I love you too", after a patient says, "I love you." But if you feel trapped, you may be too literal. Maybe Mohamed Ali dancing like a butterfly is a better model. She may be literal but you don't have to be. You don't have to be confined by literalness. You can give something from your heart or mind, but not your whole heart or mind. Or perhaps you *can* be whole-hearted in a specific way. She is after something whole. A part of a meal can be a lot if it is let in and digested. There are a lot of colours on an emotional palette. Perhaps you offer her a picnic and she wants a banquet. But she may get more from a picnic than you think.

Aner: I see now what happened. I have reduced myself to her world. The pressure on me was strong.

Mike: No wonder it was hard for you to say I love you. Of course it's a real feeling but it's also just another affect expression, part of a larger emotional palette. We're in a kind of emotional gymnasium, working the equipment, working ourselves, jumpstarting and developing ourselves. You tone up muscles. There are ways you tone emotions too. After you say I love you, you can ask, "Do you believe me? Do you feel I can feel other things too, a little of this, a little of that? A lot of this, a lot of that? Does my love for you have to be all I feel? A totally exclusive love? Of course, that is what you feel you want; the idea of a total love grips you. But you love your husband, your kid, as well as me. And I love others as well as you."

Well, maybe Rahel can take that in and work it around and maybe not. Whether she does or not, that doesn't mean you should leave your symbolic capacity behind. You can picture a world of larger and more varied and nuanced emotional possibilities. You don't have to sacrifice your sense of what is possible between people because Rahel pressures you into a tight mould. You go on upholding paradox. We are close and distant. We love and leave each other and go home to our everyday lives, and come back again. We love and keep on being therapist and patient. Our relationship is strange, paradoxical, not one thing. This confuses her. She needs to stretch, to take in complexity, that we are not one thing, that our relationship is not one thing. You can say to her, "You are getting confused because our relationship has opposites that pull on each other and you don't know what to do with them yet. You haven't dealt with a relationship like this before. It's a new kind of relationship. It takes a lot of growing into. It's not anything you're used to. Trying to make it one kind of love is like standing in front of a train."

Capacities grow over years. In terms of therapy, we're speaking of years of being together, five, ten, fifteen years. I like the notion of steeping, immersion, steeping in a therapy feeling for years, like soup on a low flame. It is not unusual for me to work with someone thirty years or more, but I am much older than you and some of my patients and I are growing old together.

My guess is that work with Rahel will take a long time. I would think in terms of the long haul and not get too bogged down in moment-to-moment crises. Do what you need to do to keep going.

The main thing is hanging in there for as long as you need to and expect that to be a long time. This kind of therapy can't be rushed. You feel pressured into rushing, but that is part of a larger process that gradually absorbs and works with that pressure.

I think, Aner, you are doing a terrific job. Rahel is connected to you. She has good feelings. She is afraid of her feelings. She is afraid of your feelings. I don't blame her. With this bond, there is a chance that in ten or fifteen years, your contact with each other will make a difference. It already has made a positive change in her life.

Second supervision: reincarnation

Aner: This is a sad story about Sarah, a young woman, twenty-eight years old, whose sister, Roni, committed suicide four years before our therapy began. When Sarah came to me she was very depressed. She was closely attached to her sister. Roni was diagnosed as schizophrenic during her service in the army. She did not show any signs of illness before she was enlisted. She became schizophrenic after eighteen months of service. After her first signs of illness the army released her from service and she stayed with her family. The family did not want to hospitalize her so they kept her closed in their apartment. Sometimes when they couldn't look after her they used to lock her in the house. One day, about four years before my patient came to me, her sister got very restless and jumped from the fourth floor to her death.

Mike: Nothing like freedom, nothing like wanting to feel free. Why didn't they want to hospitalize Roni?

Aner: They did hospitalize her for a short period of time but it was very traumatic for the family. They didn't think Roni was ill. They denied her severe mental state and they blamed the army for Roni's illness. They were devastated and yet they thought they could handle it by themselves. Sara was very close to her sister. She was two years younger. She told me that she felt they were twins. I am not sure if Sara felt that way before Roni died. They shared everything together and spent a lot of time together. Roni was the smart one, a sort of a genius, the best in her class. But socially she was timid and shy. Sara was more social but not very good at high school. She was not as ambitious as her sister. When Sara came to therapy she was depressed and sad. Life ceased. She thought that it is impossible for her to overcome Roni's death. She didn't know what to do with her life. Her parents were in profound agony and Sara distanced herself from her family. She could not expect to get any support. There was no open communication between family members.

Mike: Is this the perception in Israel that mental illness is outside society? Is there a lack of education regarding mental illness?

Aner: Yes, there is. It's a disgrace that families feel they have to hide.

Mike: It's true here, too. In general, industrial societies lack any kind of real support to educate people about what to do with mental illness. Most of the efforts are concentrated in finding the right medication rather than on finding the right human support structure. Good human support structures are needed throughout the social fabric. The case of Roni is a dramatic instance of the failure of society to educate people.

Aner: And, of course, there is the tragic story of a bright young woman who became mentally ill.

Mike: Nothing is really clear. We don't really know what happened. What we have is a variation of a common narrative, a usual narrative, the narrative of the normal. You often hear a schizophrenic say, "I was normal until this happened. I wish I could get back to the way I was before . . .". In the course of therapy it gradually comes out that things were not so good before either. The patient idealizes the time before her breakdown, an imaginary golden age before the traumatic age. An ideal feeling tries to hold personality together and persecutes it. There is no trauma-free world, no trauma-free space in real life. The idea of normalcy is largely fabricated, a spurious ideal with which to wound oneself further. An ideal one feels hopeless about, something lost forever that one never had.

It seems Sara's family found a cause, a reason for her sister's madness and suicide, in order to make things seem better than they were, to make things comprehensible. One can't believe how bad things can be. Love prevents us. One lacks a working frame of reference for digesting the fact that a traumatic age has as valid a claim on beginnings as a golden age.

Aner: There was a lot of rage within the family. It was directed against an army officer. Sara thinks that officer was too harsh on her sister and pressed her hard so that Roni would agree to extend her service. But Roni didn't want to stay in the army. Sara thought that the officer was directly responsible for her sister's illness.

Mike: I guess she wasn't able to stay. She must have felt that something bad was happening to her, something she couldn't communicate. Maybe she couldn't take it any more. Perhaps she felt in a state of semi-collapse, fault-lines of her personality giving way. The army is traumatizing, but my guess is it exacerbates personality fragility that has its own trauma history as well, trauma compounding trauma. The fact that the army was traumatizing doesn't mean the family wasn't, and the fact that the family was traumatizing doesn't mean the army wasn't.

Aner: They didn't acknowledge that. Sara had obsessive thoughts to take revenge on that officer. She considered humiliating the officer or even getting him arrested. The case was fully investigated by the army authorities but, to the frustration of Sara and her family, no charges were brought against the officer.

Mike: Did Roni become paranoid while she was serving?

Aner: Yes, she did.

Mike: What did the army do?

Aner: Well, the army does not keep soldiers who are mentally ill. They had to let her go. The family was devastated and felt the army abandoned her, caused her illness and then got rid of her. Though Roni was very ill, Sara tried to take care of her, to act as if things were normal, business as usual. She would take her out to her friends, to parties, and tried to calm her down. She did whatever she could to bring her normal sister back.

Mike: How was Sara when you first met her?

Aner: Depressed. She talked slowly, tears in her eyes, and had pessimistic thoughts about her future. On the other hand, she was doing very well in her academic studies. It was very important for her to succeed. But studying was the only thing she did. At the same time she became timid, nothing of the easy-going friendly person she was before. I saw her twice a week. Amazingly, after three weeks she suddenly changed right before my eyes. She became euphoric, happy and elated. She started saying bizarre things. She went to a rabbi who specializes in transforming secular people into orthodox Jews. A huge flock gathers every week to hear the rabbi's "scientific proofs" about the existence of God. This had a tremendous effect on Sara. Sara saw the light. She showed me the rabbi's tapes and thought she could convert me too. At that stage I was a little bit worried about this unexpected transformation from depression to euphoria, but since I saw how happy she was, and since it seemed to me natural that a young woman who lost her sister would seek spiritual meaning in religion, I did not bother myself with it too much.

But then she went another step. She was preoccupied by the idea of reincarnation. Sara's new revelation was that after one's death one's soul continues to live through other living things. No one really dies. Just before Sara came to me she went to a New Age therapist. The female therapist taught her how to meditate. To her surprise, Sara found out that this therapist was involved in reincarnation and that she could communicate with dead people through special meditative powers. Sara felt excited. She asked the therapist to communicate with Roni, but the therapist told her she did not think Sara is ready for it. Sara also found out that another teacher from her college was practising a belief in reincarnation. The fact that serious people believed in reincarnation made Sara even more convinced.

Then Sara had an insight about Roni's death. According to Sara's theory, death is not meaningless. Every death signifies some- thing. If a person sins and his soul has been transfigured into a new soul, the person who has the sinner's soul might be punished by God, even though the new soul was innocent. The innocent pays the price for the sinner. This enables the soul to purify itself. After the soul is punished it can migrate to a new creature, which is now able to enjoy a fresh start. Finding that was a dramatic point in the mourning process. Sara was so relieved when she found out that: (1) Roni's soul is still out there; (2) Roni's death had an important meaning, part of God's efforts to reorganize the puzzle of justice. It was a spiritual moment. Sara's mood dramatically improved. The only thing that kept her from communicating directly with Roni is the Jewish commandment that forbids witchcraft activity.

I was again quite puzzled by Sara's new discoveries. But at that time I was still not worried. I thought that if believing in reincarnation helps Sara to overcome her grief, then so be it. But then it got worse. She began reading the Bible for many hours. One day Sara told me that "there might be a chance" that she is part of King David's dynasty. The Messiah, she said, is already here, and that there is a chance that she is the chosen one. It was a delusional thought, but she was not utterly psychotic. Sara did not tell anyone about it except me; she kept it as a secret, realizing that people will think she is crazy. This led Sara to believe that she has to make a radical change in her life, becoming a more orthodox Jew. Sara decided to abandon her secular and sinful style of life. She felt that she has new religious duties and that she must study the Bible and prepare herself for her new missionary life. Then Sara began to think that God sent me to help her. When she read the Bible, she found signs that connect our two biblical names. In Genesis, Aner helped Abraham in his fight against the five kings. Somewhere in that chapter she found a word which reminded her of her sister's name. For Sara it was a meaningful sign. Everything became symbolic. Everyday happenings were disguised orders sent by God to her. They were meaningful riddles that she felt she had to solve. If she drove the car and someone was rude to her, then instead of yelling back she saw it as a sign from God. God is testing whether she is capable of being the Messiah.

Mike: This was not the army's fault, was it?

Aner: No. When Sara was depressed she was afraid that she would turn out to be a schizophrenic, just like Roni. She knew that schizophrenia is genetic. All her fears vanished with her new mystical revelations. Her secular parents began to worry when they noticed their daughter's preoccupation with religion. She was afraid to tell them about the reincarnation.

Mike: Why did Sara tell you about the reincarnation?

Aner: Therapy was a safe place for her. Sara wanted me to share her new revelation. She didn't want me to dismiss her ideas or to stay outside. Some quality of the relationship with her sister was transferred to me. Our relationship was sacred just as her relationship with Roni became sacred after Roni's death.

I was impressed by Sara's transformation. From a miserable, depressed, and pessimistic person she became elated, euphoric, and self confident. But I was also worried that this was a beginning of a psychotic illness. I didn't know if it would stop or escalate. It was really frightening. I sat and waited. I even prayed for Sara. What made me optimistic was that during this time Sara continued with her studies. The degree was still important for her and she was still an excellent student.

Mike: What happened then?

Aner: Her religious ideas started to fade away. I heard more about daily troubles and less about reincarnation and God. Sara spent most of her time studying for her exams. Then young men appeared in Sara's life and she began her first serious dating and her first sexual encounters. She is really good-looking, boys were interested, and she was very proud and joyful from this new start. The whole psychotic and religious content somehow faded away.

Mike: How did Sara react when you told her that you were leaving Israel for a semester?

Aner: At first she was very sad. She thought that I should not have told her about it three months in advance. For Sara it was too long. She thought I should have given her two days' notice. Why put so much pressure on her? But she got used to the idea. I promised to keep in touch with her through e-mails.

Mike: How is she now?

Aner: She misses me, and I miss her. In one of Sara's last e-mails she told me that she broke up her relations with her boyfriend. She is now thinking of another man. My impression is that she is overall in good condition. Sara is not depressed and not in her religious state of mind. What do you think about my Sara's psychotic part?

Mike: It's hard to know. One has to bear in mind that there will be vulnerability. With stress, object loss, and disappointments, psychotic thinking can emerge. So far Sara was able to get through it. She has a supportive relationship that is very important. Apparently, her sister had an extremely negative relationship with the army. It's a transference in which the army became a bad authority and rejected her personal feelings.

Bion worked with war trauma. The army felt that his job was to get the soldiers ready to fight again and Bion felt that his job was to try to *help* the soldiers, which often meant getting them back home (laughs). There is tension between institutional goals in which men fulfil functions like machines vs. concern with the personal, with soldiers as persons. When a psychotic person feels depersonalized, society often plays a role. Perhaps, too, the depersonalized psychotic individual mirrors dehumanizing aspects of society. She shows society how mad it is by what it does to her.

At the time Bion began working with traumatized soldiers, there was, at most, a weak, barely existent support system for understanding how these men were wounded psychically. Bion wrote about the conflict between authorities, who want them to get back to fighting, and the healer who wants them to come out OK. Here you have a primitive mentality in the army that does not recognize someone who is in trouble. Roni probably tried to suppress the size of her trouble as long as she could. She probably tried to show up and look as if she could do it. But then she began to weep, make little signals, saying this is too much for me, I can't do it. But the rigid authorities probably told her: toughen up, don't worry, this is nothing, only passing feelings. There was no one there to recognize that this was serious and that this woman was in trouble. It's a shame that our society is set up this way.

The scenarios that people want are at odds with each other. You have the army commanders who need the army to function and can't slow down to be sensitive to processes in which people are in trouble. They don't have the time for that. They have to see that the army functions. At the same time there are real personal tragedies. People who are too damaged and don't have the resources to function. Damage that wasn't perceived now comes to the surface. There are many divided goals, divided tendencies in social structures. The great imperative to help each other has no function at a time of war. Help gets reduced to helping each other fight, helping each other kill and win and avoid death and losing. In the long run, the wish to help each other has to win in a fuller sense. That is what the prophets talked about: let's take care of those who need help. Care for those in need, and we are all needy beings and we all ought to care. It is odd to say, but perhaps there is a growing evolutionary need or desire or demand to sensitize society to the fact that we are all human beings, that we are all people.

As for your Sara, she is vulnerable. She was probably vulnerable all her life, but a difference is that her sister didn't have an intimate support system. By intimate I mean personal, personal support, someone who supported her as a person, a real person in her own right. Roni was caught between an army that wasn't sensitive to her complaints and parents who didn't know her. The army became a bad object, telling her to forget about her feelings, to shape up and function like a soldier. It didn't care about her as a person, only as someone who had a job to do. On the other hand, her parents loved her but could not recognize her real state. They were blind to her condition. They had their image of her, which sabotaged her truth as a person. In a deep sense they were rejecting, too. The kind of acceptance they offered contained an inherently rejecting element. They could not see the real person, the individual who existed outside themselves. The army treated Roni too outside, the parents treated her too inside. There was no inside–outside balance or flow. Each tendency got short-circuited, stultified. In a way, Roni was caught between two kinds of bad objects, an unempathic rejecting object and an overly empathic blind one, neither able to recognize her real state. Neither saw Roni and her plight, her fight, her life struggle. The parents locked her up, thinking she probably would get over the illness. They granted her asylum hoping she'd get better or at least be sheltered. There was no air. They kept her illness secret. There was no social connection, no way to connect with society. No communication with the outside world. No communication with the inside world. The link between inside and outside did not develop. It deteriorated. So here you have a young woman commanded to shape up (army) or shut up (parents). So she was starved for freedom, for a real outside, a real inside. Jumping out of the window may have come as a revelation, a way out, to get out, to escape to freedom.

It was horrible. There was no place in the social fabric for recognizing and valuing Roni's personal reality. She couldn't recognize her own personal reality. There wasn't the right kind of support to mediate a fuller personal birth, a coming into her own.

Sara didn't exactly understand what was happening either. She didn't really get it. Yet somehow life led her to get help for herself. She did establish contact with the larger society in a helpful way, in ways where inner being can be personally supported and recognized and valued.

We psychotherapists may be marginal creatures, but we are by no means marginal for those who need us. For people who need us we serve a societal function in which inner and outer link up. For example, in therapy there are times when the inner beings of two people who are outside each other connect, affect each other, make a difference. The balance between inside and outside keeps shifting, but over time, a better balance is struck, and varying amalgams are tolerated in healthier ways. In spite of all our arrogance, warring schools and political manoeuvring, we create a space where people can talk to us and make contact with their inner being. This simultaneous double doubleness, or in–in/in–out flow, is a precious core capacity we play a role in cultivating. I suspect, in this, we play an evolutionary role as well, a role that spans bio–social–cultural–spiritual dimensions.

In a down to earth way, it is good for people to have a place where they can speak their worries, their fears, their secret megalomania, their craziness; soul corners which often turn out to be soul centres. What you did with Sara was: you just let her be. But it is a special letting be. It is a letting be with a supportive presence. A special supportive presence, one that values psychic life, the precious flow of subjective reality. A mixture of caring respect, respectful caring that touches the longing to grow and the need to make contact with who we are, the more that we are.

To a certain degree, you felt one with Sara. She then began to meet people: do this, do that. You gave Sara some room. In–out. Her sister never had the right kind of room. *They* (whoever became the *they*) shut her up or forced her to do what she couldn't or didn't want to do, things that did not reflect her sense of personal identity. She was suffocated or stamped on, stunted either way. Roni could not make contact with a larger society in which the self is valued. *Sara* flirted with defective contact, too. It is a kind of continuum or a matter of quality, this ability to establish, receive, use contact.

Those who do not understand therapy would be puzzled by the fact that one way you let contact grow was by shutting up and waiting. You gave the contact function time and place. This was different from the way the parents smothered contact, drenched it with unbridled concern, with blindness, including blind and blinding dread, a smothering vacuum. In therapy, Sara was getting affect food. She was fed affectively by your face, your interest, your light, your kindness, your caring, your potential usefulness as a professional, your patient hope for her. You worry that something is not going the right way. You get scared and wonder what to do and you find ways of relating to your fear, moving with it, moving through it. Sometimes you just ignore it, in tune with something else. Most basically, you work from a faith that something might happen for your patient and that *something* might be good. This kind of nuanced sea of reactivity, emotive and mental and spiritual responsiveness, was not available to your Sara's sister.

The sensitive Judge Schreber, written about by Freud, broke down when he became more successful and got married. And later in life he broke down following object loss. He broke down in face of too much and he broke down when too much was taken away. What seemed to help during his first breakdown was a psychiatrist he felt was on his side. The latter invited Schreber to family dinners, treated him like *someone*, respected him as an intelligent and interesting man. This doctor supplied a good presence, a sense of positive regard.

I'm thinking now of a certain school in Brooklyn that has terrific success. It makes kids feel good about themselves. It inflates and nurtures their sense of creativeness. It tells the kids they are great, that they can do it. It has faith in the kids and the kids feel this faith. They leave with the expectation, maybe I *can* do something. It makes them give life a little more.

Something like this happened to Schreber with his psychiatrist. The latter inflated Schreber's grandiosity perhaps, made him feel valued. The next time Schreber broke down he did not have such good luck. He was treated rather ordinarily, with no special sense of interest or value, and his condition worsened. You can see something of these two extremes in the sisters you told me about. One was in an object situation lacking this deep personal link, a situation in which she was not truly heard. The other was lucky to link up with others and a therapist who could hear her or at least try to. I suspect Sara has, or had, psychotic potential but has been able to find enough contact worth having. There probably still is a chance for psychosis, but I doubt it will be as bad as her sister. There is more air in her life, more room to breathe, more chance of meaningful affective interchange, even crazy kinds. You are supplying positive expectations in a way she can manage. You are conveying a sense that she can do things and be with people, that she is a worthwhile life form. Sara has more room than Roni to exercise life feeling.

Aner: When Sara first came to me she was depressed. She was preoccupied with all these bureaucratic things she had neglected, small things like renewing her driving licence, asking for a refund from social security, stuff like that. There were seven or eight small arrangements that she had to do. She was distressed about it, and yet couldn't bring herself to handle it. I asked Sara to bring all the papers to the session so we could do it together.

Mike: Sara's got someone in her corner. That's great. She remains vulnerable but you toned down the stimulation, you gave her your support, you gave her a helping hand.

Aner: Well, I guess I broke some psychoanalytic rules when I did that.

Mike: (laughs). One of the cruellest ideas of psychoanalysis was the idea of detached benign neutrality. It is simply not benign enough. Especially for human beings who are suffering and who are at risk. Sara was at risk. You have to do what you need to do in a particular situation. If Sara needs someone to be quiet and listen to her talk you should be quiet and listen to her talk, if she needs someone to give her interpretations you give her interpretations, or help her write letters. Your main job is to mediate between her soul and the world.

Aner: As someone who dealt a lot with psychotic states, what do you think about her involvement with reincarnation and her thoughts about being the chosen Messiah? Is it a sort of a manic defence against the sorrow and depression involving her sister's death? What should we as psychotherapists do when we encounter such a state?

Mike: Pray (laughs), hope for the best, wait it out, try to give the person support to be able to come through such states. One of the things that Winnicott says over and over is that he tries to help people go through an experience. Things will happen in the session that throw the patient off, a kind of breakdown; a breakdown that threatens to break down the session. Winnicott's concern is to keep the situation open enough for spontaneous recovery to happen. Breakdown and recovery, a basic rhythm. He supports the fact that the feelings the patient is undergoing are real, important, different sides of our nature, whether psychotic, neurotic, whatever. We try to give them time to have a voice or, in some unspoken way, become part of the background of affective aliveness. The therapist essentially plays a welcoming role. The human psyche is welcome to this place with all its hazards. We try to hold things open, see them through, a kind of implicit imperative, "Let psyche be. Let psychic movement be." There is a basic faith here, that we will survive ourselves, our impact on each other. Not only survive, but discover new psychic taste buds, taste buds that shift the quality of being. In *Coming Through the Whirlwind* I speak of "coming through an experience". John Dewey, in *Art as Experience*, talks about how difficult it is to tolerate the impact of a work of art, to undergo the experience the work asks us to. We tend to cut off the rise and fall of an experiential arc.

The depression and the mania in Sara are affect states that she was not able to go through as sides of her nature. They became persecutory, something wasn't getting digested. Important feelings were not available for use. Her very nature persecuted her. If one can hang in there long enough to go through it, then maybe something else can happen.

I had a different, but not unrelated situation. A patient was trying to close a window in her dream. She was a very sensitive person. The window was always open. It closed in a lopsided way, not fully closed. I thought about it, listened to it, and then said: "We have been working a long time together. Maybe you'll get better, you have already gotten better, but maybe it will also turn out that you are going to have to live with a lopsided window that you can't close." She felt a tremendous relief that she is going to go through life in her lopsided semi-open way. Better than too open or too closed.

Aner: What did the semi open window symbolize?

Mike: Well, it could be how things get in. She was a very sensitive lady who was extremely affected by impacts. She can do with a semi-closed window. It could be worse. The same with your Sara's mania and depression. You went through it until you became acquainted with both states well enough not to be so thrown. Of course, sometimes, if what the patient is going through is alarming, one needs to be alarmed. One may need to do something about it, hospitalization or medication, for example. However, as you sensed, Sara's psychosis was not so bad. Religion has crazy elements too, and she linked up with some of them. In a way, Sara's experience of the soul going on and on, surviving sin and death, follows the breakdown–recovery template in a semi-displaced way, a kind of aborted breakdown and recovery, so that she does not quite get all the benefit she can. The idea that her sister is not really dead because her soul is alive in someone else is not unique to her, as you point out. Many people think things like that, not just radically religious people. I doubt that anyone is exempt from psychotic processes. I think we are quite mad. The human race is quite mad. It doesn't mean that we are not also sane. We may be wonderful people doing our best but we are still quite crazy, filled with delusions. So far, it doesn't seem to have hurt that you became her twin for a time as part of a longer digestive process. Becoming one another is part of growing. At some point we snap back into place and find we are still there and have benefited. Sometimes we become more through our loss, although this is not our preferred way of growing.

CHAPTER FOUR

Afterword

Michael Eigen

A fterwords also are forewords. Like an actor coming on stage to speak with the audience after the show is over. A certain intimacy is struck, now comes the lowdown, a special sharing, just between us, no more curtains. Actor as magician with a wondrous trick: there is no other side of the curtain. That a curtain existed a few moments ago fades into imagination. And now *we* speak.

But if there is a stage, there is a show. Even if we change places, drama continues. You will be where I am and I will be where you are. A thrilling intensity. It happens all the time. In the theatre of a book it is baffling to think that only one person, the reader, is in the room.

Is it silly to say the movement of life never stops? No, it's not silly. It's wonderful. More wonderful as old age presses towards fulfilment and release. More profound as time becomes scarce. There is no more waiting. This is it. Now or never. But you discover before going over the great falls that you can't stop waiting. No matter how fast the momentum, you wait for the next moment, the not yet about to be. It is like this to the last breath.

But now, as I sit in the audience and look at the stage without curtains, I see two books of mine have appeared since my talks and supervisions with Dr Aner Govrin, and I am on the other side of seventy and wonder what is ahead. It is poignant and strange to be outside and inside the book I am adding to. To write these words puts me back onstage as actor. So, the play is not over after all. One cannot step outside the play. Perhaps *outside* is delusional. It is hard enough—and this may be our task—to find a way in.

The two books that have come out since these interviews are *Lust* and *Feeling Matters*. *Lust* is the third and last of a series of books, the other two being *Ecstasy* and *Rage*, all published by Wesleyan University Press. Lust spans many dimensions, sex, power, art (yes, there is art lust, writing lust). It trickles or blasts its way through psychic crevices and capacities of all sorts. As with ecstasy and rage, I turn lust this way and that in expressive and reflective imagination. All three of these books are fragments but, I feel, fragments with a certain emotional rigour and care. As in all my work, my desire is not to "solve" anything, but to open fields of experiencing. Perhaps my desire is to touch the thing itself, to let it touch us with all it can do. This is less putting feelings into words (I picture a noose), than mediating transmissions self-to-self. I say desire, because even death does not stop this.

Feeling Matters (Karnac) begins with a spiritual experience I had at Yosemite National Park in California. The nucleus of this park is made of giant boulders from ancient times, an awesome vision, an experience so intense I began to feel a Yosemite God. A silent God in the rocks, the great rocks going back to a time before words. You feel wordless timelessness through them. The park resonates with this profound timelessness without words. A wordless mysterious sense that brings deep relief, as if skins of self are shed. An essence that is taboo in daily life comes forward, a permeating reality that the world shies away from. One stands naked before oneself and breathes fully. One breathes pure life, full life. One breathes a holy sense at the core of one's being, of everyone's being. A sense that gives rise to rapt awe before another person, a desire to do justice to the other, to oneself, to life. A caring. Ethics grows from sensitivity, a caring will, a mutuality. It is a relief to be able to feel one wants to do good and to find the good core in the soul of one's partner.

Is this pristine state sustainable? I think in face of trauma *it* sustains *us*. We experience hints of it in a multitude of ways, e.g., in dreamless sleep, the void beneath images, or in a sense of goodness, the will to do good, a thrill in its own right, as Kant felt when he spoke of ethical perception as more thrilling than the starry night.

And yet, if we can be sure of anything, we can be sure that life is traumatizing. Trauma hits and keeps on hitting. It is part of who we are. Our very personalities have self-traumatizing aspects, which, in positions of great power, deform aspects of the larger world. Often there is a fit between childhood abuse and societal trauma, as if the two resonate and call to each other. My chapter titled "Election rape" in *Feeling Matters* dramatizes such a fit.

My patient felt raped by the 2000 presidential election in my country, in which the highest court of the land stopped the real vote count and awarded the win to a political crony. If the highest court in the land is unjust, what model is set for the rest of the populace?

Many forms of election abuse took place in order to strong-arm the winning candidate (the one who actually had more votes) into a losing position, while elevating the loser into a declared winner. My patient felt a crime against the land was committed. As in ancient times, crimes of leaders are expiated by the land as a whole. To unconscious logic, the decimation of the World Trade Center that followed was of a cloth with violence committed upon the land by election deformation. The continued political abuse gave the word "democracy" a chilling aura.

Our sessions oscillated between my patient reliving abuses of early childhood and her adult sense of societal trauma perpetuated in the present, a fit across time. Self-justifying attitudes of wounding care-takers in infancy interlock with winning lies of leaders—both try to justify impacts that might horrify.

Lies of leaders work like mummy saying, "All better", so patriotic children no longer feel the open wound. But there comes a breaking point, a point where pain reaches a critical mass and disgust and horror obtrude. As with parents, so with leaders: wounds hide in disbelief. For many, it takes time to realize that something wrong is happening. One can't believe it. The traumatizing aspect of power—whether heads of state or family—counts on the time lapse between disbelief and horror, between the horror that leads to disbelief, and the horror that awakens realization of one's condition.

Feeling Matters works with many permutations of our feeling life, from a basic sense of affirmation to a sense that we have been annihilated (at least partially so). For we manifest genuine caring as well as carry a partly decimated being. The two seem to need each other for a fuller sense of humanity.

As I hope my conversations with Dr Govrin make clear, when it comes to feelings, models that emphasize control, mastery, understanding, or transformation do not seem to have worked for society as a whole. My work asks, simply, give experiencing a chance. It is enough to try to stay with some bits of experience and see where they take us. W. R. Bion's work, like John Dewey's or Alfred North Whitehead's, each in their ways, is about enduring the capacity to experience, partnering this capacity, evolving with it. It is a potentially nourishing evolution, evolution worth pursuing. It is different from a "bully model". It practises resisting the urge to bully experience (it endures this urge, experiences it). Questioned by Dr Govrin, I speak of growing psychic taste buds, a capacity that seeks cultivation by individuals and the larger social world. Social reform is necessary but so is personal reform, again without end. To reform, to make new, to enrich, not just learning from experience, but experience as learning.